For Judith

.. How good
could you make it ?

[signature]

"If you think being an adventurer is a lot more fun than being a drudge, then Gail Blanke is your girl. Like a 21st-century Auntie Mame, she exhorts you to *live* and *act*—which is what all great adventurers do until they've convinced themselves (and everybody else) that they know what they're doing. The trick is that Gail has opened the adventurer's playbook, so if you're not a natural-born adventurer, you can become one."

—Nancy Evans, cofounder of iVillage

"Gail, everything you do inspires awe and strikes chords that are so meaningful in our lives. And now, with *Between Trapezes*, you've given us the ultimate power tools."

—Donna Kalajian Lagani,
senior vice-president and
publishing director of *Cosmopolitan*

"In this time of incredible change, more and more of us will face times of extreme uncertainty in our jobs and family lives. Gail Blanke asks us to embrace the insecurity, the struggle, the adventure of being in-between. Her book gives sound advice on how to soar on this trapeze, land gracefully, and win what we want of life."

—Helen E. Fisher, Ph.D., anthropologist
at Rutgers University and author of *The First Sex*

"I'm only thirty-nine pages into *Between Trapezes*, and I've had a Karmic Moment. You've already given me the gas to get my next big thing, Gail."

—Linda Bolliger, founder and CEO
of Boardroom Bound

"The best mental makeover you can give yourself is to read *Between Trapezes*. Gail's insight is right on!"

—David Evangelista, renowned television
personality and makeup artist

"Gail Blanke's inspiring book is about the exciting new life that awaits all of us. Her gift to you is courage, the courage to let loose and fly. She simply takes the fear out of failure. So what are we waiting for!"

—John Mack Carter, The Hearst Corporation

"Gail Blanke shows us how the periods of uncertainty we face can be fueled by imagination to help one's life take flight. She says, 'Let go, and see yourself soar!'"

—Kay Koplovitz, founder of USA Networks

"Applause all around for Gail Blanke, who provides us with a safety net of information, guidance, and empowerment as we dare to fly into the next phase of our lives—whatever that may be. *Between Trapezes* is a must-read for anyone daring to create or reinvent a career and bounce back better than ever."

—Michele Weldon, assistant professor at the Medill School of Journalism at Northwestern University and author of *Writing to Save Your Life*

"If you are not living on the edge you are taking up too much room. Read *Between Trapezes* and learn how to live with insecurity, risk, and wonder."

—Nell Merlino, creative force behind Take Our Daughters to Work Day and president of Count-Me-In for Women's Economic Independence

"Gail Blanke . . . celebrates that electrifying moment when we have let go of one trapeze and have yet to grasp the next one. She shows us how to seize the moment as our own, embrace the possibilities, and take charge of our own lives. This is a timeless message, just right for our time."

—Philip A. Glotzbach, president of Skidmore College

BETWEEN

TRAPEZES

BETWEEN TRAPEZES

Flying into a New Life

with the

Greatest of Ease

GAIL BLANKE

RODALE

Printed in the United States of America

Rodale Inc. makes every effort to use acid-free (∞), recycled paper (♻).

Poem by Danaan Parry on page 77, from *Warriors of the Heart* and *Essene Book of Days*, is reprinted with the permission of the estate of Danaan Parry.

Book design by Christopher Rhoads

Library of Congress Cataloging-in-Publication Data

Blanke, Gail.
    Between trapezes : flying into a new life with the greatest of ease / Gail Blanke.
        p.   cm.
    ISBN 1–57954–928–4 hardcover
    1. Risk-taking (Psychology)   2. Self-actualization (Psychology)   I. Title.
BF637.R57B57   2004
158.1—dc22   2004007763

Distributed to the trade by Holtzbrinck Publishers

2   4   6   8   10   9   7   5   3   1   hardcover

WE INSPIRE AND ENABLE PEOPLE TO IMPROVE
THEIR LIVES AND THE WORLD AROUND THEM

FOR MY PARENTS,
WARREN AND ISABELLE BLANKE,
WHO GAVE ME THE GREATEST GIFT
OF ALL: CONFIDENCE

ACKNOWLEDGMENTS

I HAVEN'T MET A PERSON yet who isn't—in at least some area of their life—between trapezes. And in my ongoing quest for "trapeze stories," I've met and had the great good fortune to work with some of the most wonderful, heroic, impassioned "trapeze artists" on the planet. You know who you are—and I hope you also know how much you continue to inspire me to reach out to the next and the next and the next new trapeze. Your particular story may not be in *these* pages, but there are many more pages to be written in "trapeze books" to come. So stand by.

To those of you whose stories *are* included here, there's really no way to express my gratitude for your trust, for your willingness to learn, to let go, to fly into the void with me. Thank you for allowing me to take your hand.

Richard Pine, my agent and friend, in addition to being extraordinarily smart and absurdly funny, is also a great motivator. He said, "Gail, let's get this book *out* there for God's sake. People need it *now*!" Richard is, as they say, as good as it gets. You really are, Richard.

This book would simply not exist without my collaborator, Stephen Fenichell. Stephen is not only a brilliant writer but a really wise and wonderful guy. He "got it" about *Between Trapezes* from our very first conversation. Harold Goddard, the Shakespearian scholar, said, "The destiny of the world is determined less by the battles that are lost and won than by the stories it loves and believes in." Stephen is quite simply the consummate *storyteller*. And Stephen, you not only made it good, you made it *fun*.

Stephanie Tade, my editor at Rodale, is fantastic. Her immediate response to the book proposal was unforgettable. "It's exuberant," she exclaimed the first time we met, a sentiment that captured the spirit of the venture perfectly. And Jennifer Kushnier's supportive spirit and ultra-sensitive line edits made her an absolute joy to work with.

And for all my coaches through the years from the greatest, my father, to the most embracing, my mother, to my first professional, Bob Busby, followed by Bud Wilkinson, Tom Swafford, former Avon CEO Jim Preston, Dorothy Sarnoff, Laurel Cutler, Larry Wilson, and for all of my own "players," past, present, and future, I'm immensely grateful.

And finally, getting to the heart of the matter, every trapeze artist has to have "catchers." A good catcher knows exactly when to grasp your hands—they reach out to you—not a moment too soon or a moment too late. My husband, Jim, and our daughters, Kate and Abigail, are *my* catchers. In fact, they're my everything.

CONTENTS

PROLOGUE

WE ALL KNOW THE MOMENT. The man on the flying trapeze sheds his sweeping cape and glittering costume. High in the big top, he grabs the bar, lifts off the pedestal, and then swings—one, two, three times. Craning our necks to the sky, we watch with our hearts in our throats, waiting for the big moment. Then it happens: He releases the bar. For three glorious seconds he's in midair, one bar fading behind him, the other floating forward.

Watching the trapeze artist soar through the air with the greatest of ease, we grasp that this is the most thrilling part of his act. This is where he defies gravity. This is where he flies. We understand that the moment between trapezes is a magical time, the time when anything can happen, the time when there is no past, no future, only the present. Though we may sense that this magical midair suspension is all part of the thrill, few of us ever permit ourselves to savor such sweet moments in our own lives.

Most of us don't want to be in between—and, in fact, do everything in our power to avoid those marvelous, pit-of-the-stomach, free-fall moments—usually because we worry that we might fall, and fail. If anything, lots of us can think of few things worse than being caught in between jobs, careers, relationships, lives. It's terrifying. It's embarrassing. It's shameful. It's painful. It's not where we want to be.

Yet that's precisely the place where so many of us find ourselves at the dawn of the 21st century. We live in a time of unprecedented uncertainty and insecurity. Employees who once trusted their bosses feel betrayed. Entrepreneurs who once trusted their skills and imagination now experience crushing self-doubt. Families who trusted the stock market find their retirement and college funds decimated. And after September 11, everyone who trusted that the strength and power of the United States government could keep them safe has suffered a devastating blow. Security with a capital "S" seems to be a thing of the past. Job security, financial security, personal security, and national security all appear to have flown out the window.

As an executive coach and motivational speaker, I've worked with thousands of people who have been sideswiped by life: the media executive who lost her job at the same time as her husband was diagnosed with cancer; the financial planner who lost her husband in the attacks on the World Trade Center; the real estate executive forced into early retirement. These people were hurled into the air, with no trapeze in sight.

But I have also worked with many men and women who actively yearned for their life to change, who sought out a new life but didn't quite know how to make it happen or didn't feel as if they deserved something better. Some were business people who were basically satisfied with their careers, but didn't know how to take the next step. Others knew where they wanted to go, but didn't know how to get there. Others, like the young banker who was so miserable in her position that she felt like she was in jail, were simply stuck. Another client, a lawyer, used to fantasize that she'd get hit by a car and break a leg, just so she could spend some time relaxing in the hospital. All of these people felt trapped—and sensed something worthwhile was missing in their lives. So they desperately clung to their old trapeze, losing momentum with each half-hearted swing.

With so much uncertainty pervading the world these days, almost anyone can make a strong case for being a victim, for being resigned, for sitting on the sidelines. That's what we do in difficult times—we shut ourselves down and cling to what's known.

But I'd like to suggest a sizzling, soaring, blood-pumping, pulse-racing, high-flying alternative: What if you were to *embrace* the uncertainty? What if you were to see this state of groundlessness as a good thing? What if, for the first time, you allowed yourself to not know the future, to assume the role of adventurer in your own life? Isn't the whole point of a great adventure that you don't know the outcome, and that anything can happen? Isn't that why adventures are so intrinsically thrilling?

There is, I believe, a glorious flip-side to being in-between, and I am here to help you celebrate it. Far from being periods to endure, between-trapeze moments can actually be the most invigorating, most fulfilling times of your life. When you allow yourself to not know the future, that's when you find your edge. If you can allow yourself to lean into this open space, you'll find that it's a time of stunning discovery and tremendous growth.

"It's the most wonderful, eye-opening, outside-the-box experience," says a client who is phasing out her career as a university administrator to take more art classes and pursue a career as an art therapist. "In academia, everything is subdued because we're all trying to be respectable. Now I walk out of class each night not knowing what I'll be doing next week. It really gets the juices flowing—and, paradoxically, helps me produce better results."

Unfortunately, the vast majority of us let opportunities like this pass us by. We don't embrace the uncertainty that surrounds us, and instead play it safe. We try to seem impressive to others by appearing confident about our future—by knowing who we are and what we're doing. When change comes, we want to fix it right away. We want to nail down the next job, so we go on a flurry of interviews and beam our resumes across the Internet. Or we want to find the next guy, get married again, and pretend that nothing ever happened.

We rush along in a hurry, even a panic. The result is that we move too quickly into our next life and discover that it's pretty much the same as the one we left behind. Not only do we miss the joy of being blissfully in between, we frequently miss the Big One: that wonderfully fulfilling job that uses all of our talents, that drop-dead gorgeous lover we've waited a lifetime for, that mind-blowing adventure that life was trying to hand us while we were busy trying to pin down the next tidy step. We miss the fact that the real thrill in life is not in the landing—it's in the flying. The really exciting parts of life appear when you've left the past behind but you don't yet know what the future looks like. It's in the struggle, in the becoming, during those late nights in the office when we try to pull something brilliant out of ourselves. That moment when someone asks us to work what could only be called a miracle, and somehow, we find the stuff to do it. That's the kick. Sure, the moment you get handed the award on stage is terrific, but that's not where you'll find the juice in life.

This book is all about finding that juice. And about allowing yourself to dive headfirst into your next great life without fear, without dread, without shame or embarrassment, but with a sheer joy and exuberance of living. It's about giving yourself permission to let go. To embrace uncertainty, to relish the struggle, to let go of the *need to know*. It's about allowing yourself to float in that heart-opening, mind-expanding space and improvise. It's about discovering the thrill and the joy of reinventing yourself, reinventing your life. This is not a dead time, or even a down time. This is the moment you've been waiting for your entire life.

After all, why do we love the man on the flying trapeze? It's not just that he does the impossible, soaring high above us in the circus big top—it's that he does it with the greatest of ease. That's what we love about him: He transforms himself into an entirely different creature—from man to bird, and back again—right before our eyes.

We love people like this—the people who leap from one project to the next, from one self-concept to the next, from one life to the next. People like Richard Branson, Cher, Madonna, Rosie, Oprah, and the great Flying Clintons. They make it look simple, natural, like it's no big deal. Sure they fall, but they also bounce back. We stare at them and wonder: Don't they know that they're supposed to be embarrassed? Don't they know that they fell? And if they fall, or fail, we secretly enjoy their crash-and-burn stories, because they make us feel good about the fact that we've never even tried to soar.

We think of these people as having been blessed—with a superior kind of talent, skill, or luck. Actually, these are simply people who aren't afraid of uncertainty—who in fact thrive on it. They approach every new endeavor—be it a new business, a new political campaign, or a new record tour—with a sense of curiosity and adventure, rather than fear and anxiety. They build empires not just because they want the recognition and the money, but quite simply because it thrills them. They love the process so much, they are able to separate themselves from the results. They're like inventors, always willing to experiment. They can say to themselves, "If this works out, great. If not, no problem. I'll invent something else." They work hard, do their best, and most certainly want positive results, but they don't let themselves get excessively wrapped up in a particular outcome, because they have a wider view of what it means to be happy.

Most of us have an idea of what our life needs to look like in order for it to be good. We create firm goals—married by 30, partner in the firm by 40, millionaire by 60. Many of us are devastated when we don't get that life—when savings are wiped out in the stock market, when lay-offs decimate career plans, or when Mr. Right turns out to be Mr. Wrong. We decide that we are failures simply because our life doesn't fit into a model we created decades ago.

Natural flyers don't do that. For them, the thrill is not in the trophy moments—buying the new house, landing the promotion, saying the wedding vows. All those glittering prizes are just gravy. For flyers, the fun comes from negotiating the deal, not signing the paper; making the movie, not winning the golden statuette. When they fall, they bounce back quickly because they never took it very seriously. They have a sense of levity, an intuitive understanding that it's all just a game. They aren't burdened by a narrow definition of success, which, paradoxically, makes them more successful.

This book will show you how to bring that same sense of buoyancy into your life. It will enable you to make changes and reinvent yourself in ways that will truly propel your life forward. You'll get the tools that will help you soar into your next life, and the one after that, and the one after that. So step into the big top with me. Climb up the pedestal far above the crowd. Look out at that great, vast, beautiful unknown and take my hand.

We've got some flying to do.

DEFINING MOMENTS

IT WAS SEPTEMBER 14, 2003, and my husband, Jim—the real cook in our family—had just whipped up one of his marvelous pasta dishes. Meanwhile, in the dining room, I had just picked up a glass of chilled pinot grigio in one hand and was about to light a candle with the other when suddenly a staccato series of explosions rocked our apartment building. You could not only hear them, you could *feel* them, shaking the very foundations of our apartment building on Manhattan's Upper East Side—or so it seemed.

"Jim! Jim!" I shouted, as our golden retriever, Molly, began jumping all over me in a panic. Still jittery two years after September 11, and convinced that we were once again under attack, I instinctively ran away from the window and into the kitchen, where Molly, Jim, and I lay flat on the kitchen floor and waited for the next explosion to blow. The first thing I could think to do was to reach for my cell phone to call our older daughter, Kate, who was somewhere in downtown Manhattan on her way to a college reunion. Abigail, our younger daughter, was safely away at college, so I didn't feel the need to call her—at least not right at that moment. After leaving a message on Kate's cell phone asking her to call us back immediately, we listened intently for the sound of the shocks.

As we lay there like soldiers ducking for cover, I could have sworn that those muffled explosions sounded more like gunfire than bombs. This oddly comforting thought eventually compelled me to stand up to size up the situation. I headed—tentatively, gingerly, cautiously—into the dining room, accompanied by Jim and Molly. All three of us stood at the window for a few seconds, looking out onto our terrace, which faces east across the perpendicular skyline of upper Manhattan. Deciding that it was probably safe to walk out onto the terrace, I gazed down into the street. Quite a few people had gathered down there on the sidewalks, oddly enough, and most of them seemed to be gazing curiously skyward, prompting me to look up too. Then I saw them: the brightly colored shimmering shapes of fireworks exploding in the sky, reflected in our apartment windows. My first response was outrage. How could "they"—the authorities, the powers-that-be—have permitted such a frivolous display to shatter our fragile composure, at such a sensitive time? It was only a few days after the second anniversary of September 11, and this was New York City. No more than a beat or two had elapsed, after the first wave of anger subsided, when I felt an enormous sense of relief. No, we were not being attacked, we were not being bombed, we were not being shot at, we were not being killed. Instead, our great city of New York, in its infinite wisdom, had insensitively permitted a fireworks celebration of the 150th anniversary of the founding of Central Park to go forward, apparently unaware that a pyrotechnic display might strongly resemble—sonically speaking—an all-out terrorist attack.

Every summer fireworks go off over Central Park when the New York Philharmonic plays the *1812 Overture*, and no one thinks anything of it. Molly, in fact, has long since grown accustomed to the sound of the pinwheels and roman candles and scarcely lets the artillery faze her. But this night was September 14, and was therefore not like other nights. Once Jim and I finally sat down to our pasta and I was at last able to pick up that no longer so deliciously chilled glass of wine, I began to think more consciously about what had just happened to us.

One of things that had happened to us was that the authorities had failed to take into account the state of peoples' nerves two years after a traumatic event. Another thing that had happened to us was that a form of mass hysteria had taken hold, as hundreds of people in the surrounding buildings flowed into the streets, all looking for help, all panic-stricken, all intently convinced that the world—or at least the city—was going up in smoke and that apocalypse was now. A third thing that had happened was more psychological, and was something with which I am intimately familiar. Based on past experience, we had automatically leapt in our minds to the worst-case scenario. Something intended to be celebratory, something intended to be fun—fireworks in the park—had, under these exceptional circumstances, taken on a new, nightmarish tone.

This was yet another example of the reality that while none of us can change the *facts* of our lives, we can change the *interpretations* we place on those facts. And we can do so in all sorts of ways that have the power to liberate as opposed to enslave us. A couple of weeks later, I gave a speech to a group of executives at Citicorp in New York. With the traumatic incident of September 14 still fresh in my mind, I advised my audience,

> Sometimes it takes a crisis, in a country or in a company, for you to find out *who* you are, *what* you stand for, and what you stand *against*. Sometimes it takes a crisis to really learn what you're made of and what you want to become, and to create. Sometimes it takes a crisis for you to find out what you're really passionate about, and to summon up the energy to create a vision for how good life could be. Those times of crisis are our defining moments.

I asked the assembled executives to stop for a few seconds and think about a defining moment in their own lives, and to look back at that moment, and *own* it. Everyone has a moment when you decided: a moment when you said, "Here's how it's going to go;" a moment when you stood up for something; a moment when you said "yes;" a moment you said "no." It could be the moment you decided to have the baby. It could be the moment you decided to stay, or decided to leave. It could be the moment you drew a line, or stepped up to the plate, or laid it all on the line—or erased one, if that's what needed to be done. These are the moments of your own personal heroism, which define who and what you are. Lay claim to these moments, which embolden you to step into your power. Those moments, I went on, form a platform from which one can spring into a new life. Those moments, I insisted, can provide us with the energy, the focus, and the courage we need to ride our own particular beams of light to the castle we create in the sky.

I told them about Walt Disney, and how when he created his theme parks, he instructed his crews to "build the castle first." With Cinderella's palace clearly in sight, Disney knew that his employees could always take inspiration from that fairy-tale castle whenever they were tired or discouraged, when they were digging trenches for the castle, when it was hot, when the mosquitoes came out to play.

If you can feel the magic, you can go the distance. Disney understood how a gorgeous vision can propel us forward, how when we are laboring in the swamps and the ditches of our own lives, we can look up at the horizon and see our dream castle, our better life, shimmering and glittering in the distance, pulling us forward and upward.

Facts, I told my audience matter-of-factly, are "measurable, demonstrable, and inarguable." But all of us have a natural tendency to sort of smoosh these facts together in our minds in such a way that the neat conceptual packages we assemble do not always so neatly accord with objective reality. Just as Jim and Molly and I, along with a few hundred other gullible souls in our neighborhood, had leapt to certain erroneous conclusions on that harrowing night in September, we all tend to string together masses of facts and fiction and put them into neat little boxes that are highly plausible, yet at the same time subjective *interpretations* of reality.

None of this would really matter so much if we didn't then take those interpretations and use them as the basis for decisions, actions, and opinions. "Wars are fought, stocks markets move up and down, divorces are adjudicated, and decisions in life and business are made every day based on *interpretation*, not fact," I assured my audience of corporate executives. I then asked these high-powered people to envision the possibility that there might be better, higher, more empowering interpretations to be made of the facts that might help us leap to new heights and create entirely new selves. Contrary to popular perception, we do not need to live our lives passively, like watching a movie or TV. *We*, in fact, write and direct our own movies. *We*, in fact, get to decide what reality is. *We*, in fact, possess the power inside us to edit and revise reality as we see fit and to create a new reality that helps us to realize our intrinsic greatness.

Some people—we call them heroes (or trapeze artists)—know how to make the defining moments of their lives count, and they become sterling examples of character. On November 18, 1985, as described in a *Houston Chronicle* article, the superb violinist Itzhak Perlman played at New York's Lincoln Center. Seeing Perlman walk out on stage is in itself an incredible sight. As a child, he was stricken by polio, and he walks with braces on both legs, perpetually propped up on crutches. The audience watched with a mixture of awe, pity, and admiration as Perlman laboriously, majestically stepped up to his chair, sat down on it, and very slowly and deliberately set his crutches down on the floor before undoing the clasps that bound the braces to his legs. Tucking one foot back and extending the other forward, he slowly and deliberately bent down and picked up the violin and tucked it under his chin. Nodding to the conductor, he began to play.

A few seconds later, a violin string snapped. As the *Chronicle* described this unforgettable scene, "It went off like gunfire across the room. There was no mistaking what that sound meant. There was no mistaking what he would have to do. People who were there that night thought the same thing to themselves: '. . . He would have to get up, put on the clasps again, pick up his crutches and limp his way off stage to either find another violin or else find another string for this one.' "

Instead, he waited a moment, closed his eyes, and signaled to the conductor to strike up the music again. Without missing a beat, he picked up precisely from where he had left off. That night, even for Itzhak Perlman, was not like other nights. That night, he played with such extraordinary passion and power and purity that he transported us all to a place where it is actually possible to play a major symphonic work for violin with *just three working strings*. Such a place, of course, does not exist in reality. But that night, Perlman made a conscious decision not to know that, or pay attention to it. That night, he decided not to behave in accordance with the observable facts. According to the *Chronicle*, you could actually see him modulating, changing, and recomposing the piece in his mind so that it could be played with three strings. At one point, in fact, it almost sounded as if he was detuning the strings to extract entirely new sounds from them—sounds never before created.

When he finished the piece, a split second of silence filled the hall before people spontaneously rose and applauded and laughed, some cheering, some screaming, some weeping. In response, Perlman smiled, wiped the sweat from his brow, raised his bow to quiet the audience and softly said to the now quiet room, "You know, sometimes it is the artist's task to find out how much music you can still make with what you have left."

A broken violin string is, of course, not a major crisis, even for a concert violinist. But it can be a significant setback, from which only the greatest musician could possibly have snapped back with such grace and verve. "Sometimes it takes a crisis," I told my audience at Citicorp, "to make us know who we are and what we stand for." It doesn't have to be the Cuban Missile Crisis. It doesn't have to be rushing into a burning building to save a child. It could even be somebody else's crisis. I told them a story from my own life that illustrated the fact that sometimes it's a seemingly small thing. One day about two years ago, I was waiting on Madison Avenue, praying for a cab. It was pouring down rain, and I was wearing a pair of shoes that even on sale I had had no business buying. I had to get a cab or the shoes would be ruined. Magically, a cab appeared. We sped up Madison Avenue and as we stopped at a red light I glanced out the window and saw a young man in this thirties holding a pretty big dog wrapped in a blanket. He looked stricken. After the light changed, and the cab continued racing up Madison Avenue, I said to the driver, "Did you see that guy with the dog?"

"Yeah," he said, shooting me a curious glance in the rearview mirror.

"We've got to pull over," I said, and he did. Getting back out into the rain, I told him, "Stay right here, and whatever you do, don't let anyone take this cab. I bet they need to go to the Animal Medical Center."

"Okay, okay," he said, and trusting that he would do as I asked, I ran two blocks back through the pouring rain and found the guy with the dog. "I've got your cab for you," I said, "come on." Together we ran back up to where, to my astonishment, we saw the taxi driver standing outside his cab in the pouring rain, holding the door open for his new passengers. They got in and away they went. Needless to say, the shoes were never the same.

Other defining moments, by contrast, are truly heroic. Since

September 11, I have often thought of the last moments of Lisa Beamer's husband, Todd, who led the attack on the hijackers that caused the flight bound for the Pentagon to crash into a Pennsylvania meadow instead. Having grasped that he could do something not to save himself or his fellow passengers but the lives of the other potential victims on the ground, Todd Beamer sprang into action. Let's think of the moment he called out to his fellow passengers in the uprising, "Let's roll!"

And they did.

If that's not a defining moment—not just for Todd Beamer, but for all of us—I don't know what is. It was a moment for which everything in his life had been a rehearsal. That is the shout of the man on the flying trapeze as he leaps out into the void. These are not times in which it pays to sit back and wait for the dust to settle, for everything to return to normal. This *is* our new normal. That was a new normal evening when Jim and I and our dog flipped out on September 14, a new normal evening in which the brave spirit of Todd Beamer was as important an inspiration as Charles Lindbergh and the *Spirit of St. Louis* were to the Americans of 1927.

Let's take a look at a defining moment in the life of Annika Sorenstam, the great woman golfer, who had a vision of qualifying and competing in the 2003 PGA Colonial Invitational Tournament. To her delight, she did qualify, and she became the first woman to compete in that tournament since Babe Didrikson Zaharias nearly forty years before. Many of the men who had been planning to play that day were not necessarily thrilled by

Annika's decision to compete. In fact, a couple of them were graceless enough to accuse her of having a "big ego," as if that were such a terrible thing in a pro golfer! But she went ahead anyway, shrugging off the catcalls, under a degree of pressure that I can only imagine was extraordinary. On her first day out on the links, she played not merely well, she played *brilliantly*. But on her second day out, she lost her edge, and with it her place in the tournament.

Did Annika Sorenstam lose her defining moment? No, she defiantly won it. Wiping a tear from her eye and standing straight and tall, she told the world with a smile on her face that she wouldn't have missed the chance to play in that tournament for anything. The vision she had had of herself—her personal castle—had been built in her mind. Not that winning—and beating all of those men—wouldn't have been nice, but in the end, it was beside the point. Why did people find even the act of watching Annika so thrilling? One might as well ask why people get a thrill out of living through hurricanes, or riding rollercoasters. Because win or lose—and not necessarily with the greatest of ease—we wanted to see Annika *soar* on her personal trapeze.

I'll share with you a few defining moments in my life, if you promise to write the details of *yours* down: I want you to *own* them, so that you can summon up in the future some of the courage you have already displayed in the past. You might recall the moment in Thornton Wilder's *Our Town* when a woman named Emily, who seems to have died while giving birth, is given a chance to pick a single moment in her life to relive. She picks her tenth birthday, and when she sees herself as a child, when she sees how cavalier she was and seemingly oblivious to the birthday hug of her father, the "Happy birthday, darling" from her mother, she bursts into tears, not so much out of sadness as out of frustration at the fleetingness of life.

"Can't we just stop for a moment and realize that life is *happening?*" she asks, and solemnly swears to herself, "I will never *not* know this moment."

I was the same age as Emily on her birthday when my grandfather—my mother's father—passed away. My grandparents lived in Florida, and I knew that grandpa had been sick for some time when my parents flew down to visit them. The night my parents returned to Bay Village, Ohio—the little town on Lake Erie outside Cleveland were I grew up—the very first thing I asked my father, a split second after he'd walked through the door, was, "How's grandpa?"

"Let's go upstairs," he replied, and I could instantly tell that something was wrong. "Is grandpa *okay?*" I insisted.

My father took one kind look at me and said, "Actually, he's absolutely fine."

"Oh my god," I shouted, knowing full well what that meant, throwing my arms around him. Like Emily in *Our Town*, I resolved never to forget that moment for as long as I lived. I can distinctly recall, for example, feeling shocked that the song they played over the radio that night, "Lavender Blue," was the same song that they'd played the night before. Didn't the people on the radio *know*, I asked myself, that everything had utterly changed? How could they not realize that in light of my grandfather's death—that unthinkable change—that the music had to change too?

A couple of years later, when I was twelve, I accompanied my mother to a department store in downtown Cleveland to buy a party dress. I saw a brightly colored number that had a ruffle and a sash, and I desperately wanted my mother to buy it for me. She took one mildly horrified look at the dress and stage-whispered to the saleswoman, "She's more of the tailored type."

I froze in my tracks. What on earth did *that* mean? Was it some sort of a *code*? Did that really mean, in that secret language these adult ladies undoubtedly shared, "not the pretty type"?

Many years later, still troubled by my mother's off-the-cuff remark, I asked her what she had meant by it. Shocked that I should have remembered the incident at all, which was admittedly vague in her mind, she replied in amazement, "Why *darling*, I meant that you were the *elegant* type! That dress was so tacky!"

We swim in a sea of interpretation. Something trivial happens, and we—being only human—instantly imbue it with meaning, not always correctly. We are meaning machines, causing meaning and interpretation to constantly blend together, often in ways that are harmful to our cause, and that cause us to dowse out our own fires. Are we "the silent type," "the tailored type," or, God forbid, "the racy type"?

These are our negative defining moments, the opposite of the heroic moments of a Todd Beamer, an Annika Sorenstam, or an Itzhak Perlman. These are the moments in which we let other people define us, instead of letting those moments define us in ways that enrich us as opposed to diminish us.

One night when I was twenty-one and a senior at Sweetbriar College in Lynchburg, Virginia, the phone in my dorm room rang. Picking it up, I had been hoping the call was from a boy I liked at the University of Virginia and was a bit disappointed to hear my mother's voice on the other end of the line. "Hello, darling?" she said. She sounded warm, but a little stilted and strange. "Is there anyone there with you?"

"No," I said, finding the question a little odd.

"I want you to go get Nerissa," she said, softly but firmly, "and I'll wait here on the phone."

Thoroughly confused by this request, I ran into the hall and began shouting for my former roommate and still closest friend. I knew I was annoying a number of other girls in the lounge who were trying to study, but I also knew that somehow this was important. Rousting Nerissa from her room, I told her that my mother wanted to speak to her, and I put her on the phone.

"I've got something really hard to tell Gail," my mother said to Nerissa. "I want you to stay by her side. Do you understand?"

Then I got on the phone, and my mother said, "Something has happened."

My body started shaking uncontrollably, because I already knew what she was about to say. I dreaded hearing it more than anything in the world.

"There's been an accident," she went on. Not long before, I'd had a premonitory dream that the accident involved my beloved older brother, a Navy pilot. And I had actually dreamed that I demanded of God, "Take *me*, please. Take *me*, not him!"

"Is he okay?" I was shouting, but I couldn't stop myself.

"Gail," she said, "we will never lose him."

That one very important sentence set the tone right from the start for everything that followed, for years to come. The point of this defining moment was that it was not about death, it was about life. It would not be about wallowing in the pain of the past, but about moving forward into the future. Forever after, our family would refer to the event as "the accident," and we very purposefully never thought of it so much as a loss as that he was still there with us, every minute of the day, forever, as long as we lived.

I later learned that my mother had been calling from the airport in Washington, D.C., where the Navy had somehow managed to track my parents down as they passed through on their way home to Ohio. I would never not know that moment, I resolved, like Emily in *Our Town*. That was the moment that my parents taught me not about death, but about life, and about how there is a right way and a wrong way to live. That moment, I knew then, would be not an end, but a beginning, and everything afterward would be different. That moment became my great motivator, propelling me forward. It was a moment for which, strange as it sounds, I would be forever grateful.

PUTTING YOURSELF
ON THE PEDESTAL

Let's think of another defining moment. This is the moment you stand high in the circus big top, gazing down at the sea of small faces and the vast open space spread out before you. The future is completely open, your possibilities limitless. Your old concepts and beliefs about yourself are suspended. You have a glimpse of just how large your life could be—the people you could meet, the places you could go, the twists and turns your life could take.

You see it all, but you're also justifiably scared. The life you now have may not be perfect, but it's what you know. How could you possibly risk what you have—a steady paycheck, a regular date to friends' weddings—and hurl yourself into the void? How do you maintain your inspiration during all of those times when you slip and fall, or the days when you just don't feel like flying?

An inspiring vision enabled Eileen Roper Ast to sail through one of the most challenging times of her life. In the spring of 2001, Ast thought she had it all. She had a great job as director of communications for a large magazine conglomerate. She lived in a lovely home in Connecticut with her husband and thirteen-year-old son. But in the spring of 2001, things began to fall apart. Ast's company was purchased by another publisher, and she was let go. Then her husband was diagnosed with bone cancer.

Ast was overwhelmed. How would her family survive financially? How would she resume her career while taking on a host of new responsibilities—driving her husband to his treatments, quizzing the doctors about his condition, fighting with insurance companies?

"I was in such a panicky state," Ast recently recalled. "I had never not worked—it was part of who I was. So I had this anxiety and resentment that I had to take care of my husband." When Ast came to one of my Lifedesigns workshops the following August, she was frustrated and angry, her head spinning with all of the bad things that had happened to her. She was virtually weighed down by it all. But she decided she should give it her best shot.

"I decided I would suspend any thought of what I *should* be doing," she says. During the first day, Ast was very thoughtful and quiet—something was stirring. Through exercises and discussion, Eileen began expressing her desire for a new direction. She was tired of corporate communications. "I didn't want to keep doing what I was doing. I knew that if I had to write another press release I'd jump off a building," she says. As Ast quietly outlined her passions and dreams, she realized that her heart was in the nonprofit world. "I realized that I wanted to make a difference in a professional way." As she considered her work experience, it slowly dawned on her that she had the right skills. She was already serving on the board of a nonprofit organization, and she had also worked for five years as a Montessori teacher.

"I realized I had already learned about the intricacies of running a not-for-profit, and I also realized that my strength was leadership. So I asked myself, 'What would give me the most satisfaction at this time of my life? Who do I want to be now?'"

When it came time to announce our plans for the future, Ast said very quietly, almost shyly, that she'd like to run a nonprofit organization. We all agreed we could see her doing that.

"Really?" she said, pleasantly surprised. It took a few minutes for the reaction to sink in, but then she sat up straight and said, "Well, that's what I'm going to do. I'm going to run a not-for-profit organization."

Mind you, Ast didn't say that she wanted to maybe transition into nonprofits, or that she was hoping to find a public-relations position in nonprofits. She said she would be the CEO. "It was very brazen," recalls Ast. "Before I went to the workshop, I didn't know what I was going to do—I just knew what I was moving away from. But it had been percolating for a while, and sometimes you need the right tools to bring it to the surface."

As soon as Ast declared her intentions, I could see the tension drain from her face; she looked years younger. "It was still scary to say it out loud, because I was making it so public," says Ast. "I was a middle-aged woman saying that I wanted an entirely different way of life, that I wanted to express myself in a completely new way."

A skeptic might say, "Big deal. Anyone can stand up before a touchy-feely workshop and announce that they will be an astronaut, a movie star, the king of France—that doesn't mean that they will do it." That's true—stating your intentions is merely the first step. But it's an absolutely critical step, because it's the time when you announce to the world—and to yourself—that *you* are taking the reins.

You Get To Decide

Most people don't understand that they get to decide how their life is going to go. But it's true. *You* get to decide just how brilliant your life will be. *You* get to decide everything.

Most of us live our lives as if we're watching a movie—one that someone else is writing, producing, and directing. We sit back with our popcorn and Jujubes and say, "I wonder how this will turn out?" "Will she get the job?" "Will he get the girl?" "Will they live happily ever after?" We sit in the dark and wait for the answer. Well, guess what? The answer lies with you. You're Sam Goldwyn. You're in charge. You always have been, and you always will be.

Many of my clients believe that the universe has made up its mind about them, that the die has long since been cast. They say, "That's just the way it is, and that's just the way I am, so there's no point in trying to change it."

But that simply isn't the case. There's no "way it is." There's only the way you *say* it is.

Of course, Ast's life didn't miraculously change the day she walked out of my workshop. She was still between trapezes. But now she had a vision. Now she had a point of light. She had seen the new trapeze; she had built the castle. That beautiful vision of her dream job kept her on track through some very shaky times.

"It wasn't all upbeat," says Ast. "It was a very frightening time. I was very insecure, because I didn't know how long it would last. My son would ask me the very questions I was asking myself: 'Mom, why did you leave your last job? Will you ever get another one?'"

Ast received a couple of very attractive job offers in corporate communications. "They sounded terrific, but they were more of the same." These offers were actually the safe corporate trapeze she'd already been swinging on, merely disguised to look like the one out in front of her. Different companies, slightly different titles, but ultimately jobs that would keep Ast in the same lifestyle. Because she had a clear vision of her new life, Ast could resist the safe bets—even in the midst of illness, uncertainty, and her child's anxieties about their future. She wanted to swing to a brilliant new trapeze, not simply grab any old lifeline.

Even during her darkest hours, Ast committed to doing one thing a day that she could feel good about—whether it was joining a networking group, contacting an executive search firm, or doing Internet research on not-for-profits. To keep a hand in the professional realm, she accepted an unpaid position as president of the New York Women in Communications Foundation.

Ast says the job enabled her to maintain her sense of herself as a professional. As she sat in meetings next to some of the top women in her profession, she saw that they weren't treating her like an unemployed loser. They treated her like a peer, like the president of a large and influential organization.

"There comes a time when you say, 'If I am ever going to do it, I need to do it now,'" she says. That was her defining moment, when she made her decision to embark on this new career path, the moment after which nothing would ever be quite the same.

The first part of her redefinition was seeing that there were whole sides of herself that were shut down because she had been so busy with work. "When you're working all the time, you're lucky if you get near your spirituality," she later recalled. Now she could. She started taking yoga classes, getting massages, and reading books on spirituality. She also became more involved in her community, which, before, had just been a place between the commuter train station and her house. But with her newfound free time, Ast joined the board of the Norwalk Symphony. She also dusted off her old teaching credentials and started substitute teaching. "I really enjoyed getting more involved in the community, getting to know more people in my town, and seeing my neighbors socially," she says. "I started feeling whole again."

Instead of feeling resentful that her husband's illness coincided with her layoff, Ast began to feel grateful that she had the extra time to spend with him.

"We both learned about trust and love on a level that we had never experienced before, because we were both so raw. I was able to finally say, 'This was supposed to happen.' "

Then, in November, one of Ast's networking contacts sent her a posting that he had found on the Internet: The American Montessori Society was looking for an executive director. Ast *knew* in her heart of hearts that this was her job. With the help of an executive recruiter, Ast wrote a killer presentation, outlining the job requirements on one side, and her skills on the other. In the slot that said that the job required a master's degree, which Ast did not have, she outlined her life experience and Montessori training. "It was a really impressive document, and I heard back very quickly," she says.

By February, Ast was one of three candidates still being considered for the job, and she was asked to interview with the

American Montessori Society board in Washington, D.C. Ast would be given five minutes to tell the sixteen-member board why she should get the job, and she asked me to help her develop her pitch.

Of course, we wanted to talk about her qualifications, but believe it or not, that's not what I wanted to emphasize. Most people approach job interviews with a degree of anxiety. "Will they like me?" "Will they see how good I am?" So they barrel into the interviewer's office and pummel their prospective employer with information—every project they initiated, every contact they've nurtured, every employee-of-the-month award they've received. Heck, they'll give up their second-grade report card if they think it would help. They think that employers want data, charts, and numbers verifying their merit, but that's not what really gets jobs.

Obviously, an impressive résumé is important, but the truth is, employers aren't all that interested in what we've done in the past—they want to know what we'll do for them in the future. That's why I urge my clients to ask their prospective employers to describe their vision for their company. If anything were possible, what would they love to have happen? Ast talked to former colleagues and other people in the Montessori world, and through her research learned that the American Montessori Society was looking for someone to put Montessori back on the map—it had been popular in the sixties and seventies, but then interest had waned.

Ast realized that the Montessori Society needed someone to bring modern marketing techniques into the organization—it needed to be run more like a business than a nonprofit. With her corporate communications background, Ast had the perfect credentials.

But before Ast told the board about all of the great things she had done for her former company, she talked about the Montessori Society, showing them that she understood and respected their tradition, explaining why she believed in the organization, and why she was passionate about Montessori. Then she built the castle: She showed them a glorious image of what the organization could become. She detailed her strategy for bringing Montessori into the twenty-first century and presented her interviewers with examples of past projects that proved she was qualified for this task.

That's very different from bursting into a room and saying, "Aren't I great? Look at all that I've done." Ast's conversation was focused on the Montessori Society and how her talents were directly relevant to it. More important, Ast *showed* how the Montessori Society's vision meshed with her own personal vision, and how passionate she was about using the talents that she developed in the for-profit world for a higher good.

"I told them that this position was the culmination of my entire career. It brought together the pieces of everything I've done for my entire professional life," she says. I'm sure the other people who interviewed for this position were very talented and had many great qualifications. But Ast gave them something extra—she showed them *their* new trapeze: "I can see who you are, and I want to take you even further. I want to be the person who makes you thrive."

Is it any surprise that Ast got the job?

If Ast hadn't allowed herself to be between trapezes and have that period of discovery, she would never have realized the possibilities inherent in this new life. She needed the exploration time to get outside of her usual life and discover what she really loved. Not only did Ast get her dream job—and a husband who, mercifully, is in remission—she now has an expanded sense of possibility. She took a terrible situation—losing a job—and turned it into one of the best things that has ever happened to her. Eileen lost her job and found another in an entirely different career in less than a year. That remains a testimony to her exceptional focus on building her castle and inventing a new life for herself. She was able to fly, because she knew where she needed to land.

Honor Your Previous Flights

Your flight of fancy might seem like a daydream—sure you'd love to nab that lucrative and creatively fulfilling job, marry that fantasy person, and raise beautiful, smart, well-adjusted children. But what makes you think you can achieve such heights? Quite simply, *because you've done it before.*

Flying is scary because we can never remember all of the times when we've soared before—making the state finals in the high school tennis tournament, landing that first job, standing up and telling someone "no" for the first time. These are the times when we sailed into the void and came out a different person. The trouble is, as soon as we accomplish something like this, we just move on to the next thing. We don't stop to acknowledge what we've done.

I'm guilty of this, too. Recently, I spoke before the National Association of Women Business Owners in Los Angeles. The audience gave me a standing ovation, and I was on top of the world. For a day and a half. Then I started thinking about new challenges—a pending TV project, an upcoming speech, a particularly demanding coaching assignment. After a few days, my beautiful moment of flying high felt like a distant memory, almost as if it had happened to someone else.

That's the real challenge in life—to remember the many affirmations that life gives us. I'm not talking about looking into a mirror and telling yourself how great you are. I'm talking about examining the facts. The sad truth is, negative experiences usually have more lasting effects than positive ones. When we fall— the marriage ends, the bank rejects the mortgage application, the "killer" presentation is met with blank stares and deafening silence—we inflict harsh judgments on ourselves. We let those moments define us.

Don't let those moments define you.

Instead, we need to define ourselves by the moments when we *fly*—the time when we got the job, nailed the report, or made a difference in a child's life. We need to view those moments when we slip as the necessary steps to taking flight. Most of us don't come close to doing this. In fact, we'll even call positive experiences "useless" if they don't have immediate relevance to our goals. We don't see that raising three children provides great lessons in management or that waiting tables requires superior people skills. But when you honor your past, you start to see the myriad ways that your skills and experiences can serve you.

ONE MORE DEFINING MOMENT

Several years ago, I was fortunate to be invited by the *Oprah Winfrey Show* to talk about my new book, *In My Wildest Dreams*. Before the taping began, one of the producers met me in the green room and explained that they were taping opening segments for several other shows. Before I went on, Oprah would come to the green room and we would chat for about ten minutes. Then I'd go to the set, where there would be two big yellow chairs. Oprah would sit in one, and I'd sit in the other. We'd talk to the audience a bit, and then Oprah would start the show. "What I really want is energy, Gail, okay?" said the producer. "Energy. Badda-bing, badda-bang, badda-boom. Got it?"

She left the green room, and I sat there for an hour and a half. By myself. I remember wishing that I'd brought my book with me, so I could read it and remember what in God's name I had to say. *Whatever made me think I could do this?* I wondered, apprehensively watching the monitor. Oprah said that she hated her hair. And why, for that matter, while she was thinking about it, did she ever decide to wear this thick gray and yellow striped sweater? It made her look fat, she said. She also mentioned that she had bean soup for lunch, and you know how that makes you feel. You know how much the audience loves it when Oprah says what everyone else is thinking about themselves? But for me, all I could think about was how my energy was continuing to plummet. When it was time for me to go on, the producer explained that they were running late, so Oprah wouldn't have time to come back and chat. I walked out onto the set, where Oprah reclined in one of the big yellow chairs.

"Hi, I'm Gail," I said.

She shook my hand, looked at the director, and said three words that are now needlepointed onto a pillow in my office.

"Get the bench."

Huh? *Get the bench?* I wondered what on earth that meant, just as many years before, I'd wondered what did my mother mean when she said I was "the tailored type." And of course, being only human, my mind leapt to the worst-case scenario. This was undoubtedly some TV updated version of the old vaudeville saying, "Get the hook." Or this was probably producer lingo for, "I'm not doing this show with this chick."

While I continued to ponder these imponderables, growing more anxious and fretful by the minute, they took away the yellow chairs and Oprah said, "You sit on the bench. I'm going to sit in the audience."

The producer came over and, trying to pep me up, whispered, "I want a lot of energy, Gail. Badda-bing, badda-bang, badda-boom."

My whole life passed in front of me in about a second and a half. What on earth was I doing here anyway? What on earth ever made me think I was good enough to do an entire hour of *Oprah*?

Desperately determined to get my strength back, I asked myself the following questions: What am I doing here? What am I committed to? What am I out here for? I could have been committed to being right about the fact that it's not very nice to just put a woman on a bench. But I knew that in reality I was committed to making sure that everyone in that room, and everyone in that television audience, came away with a new sense of what was possible in their lives.

So what did I have to make "Get the bench" mean in order to make good on my commitment? I decided—because I realized that I got to decide what it meant—exactly what it meant, in this moment, now. "Get the bench" meant "Oprah trusts you. Go ahead, Gail. Take the show." If Oprah trusts me, who am I not to trust myself?

And so I did.

Within moments, both Oprah and I were out of our seats and into the audience, keeping not only my commitment but hers: that people leave the show with a new sense of what was possible in their lives. In the end, Oprah embraced me as only Oprah can. An embrace from Oprah is a defining moment.

But I had learned something important, a lesson that you can say a hundred times but that you have to live before it really sinks in. Ultimately, it didn't matter what Oprah thought "Get the bench" meant. It mattered what *I* made it mean.

We get to create our own defining moments, which clarify who we are in ways that make us better and stronger and smarter and happier than we have ever felt before in our lives. It was I who left that room that day more aware of the possibilities out there in my own life. That is why I am writing this book—and doing my best to keep living it, ever minute of the day. We all have our defining moments, which tell us who we *really* are, not what other people want us to be.

Exercise One: See the New Trapeze

Ask yourself, "If absolutely anything were possible, what would I love to have happen?" Not what would be nice, or what seems reasonable. Forget reasonable. *Think big.* What would I love to do? Whom would I love to be? How good could it be? Write the answer to these questions in a spiral-bound notebook that you use exclusively with this book. Your "Flight Log" will be critical to helping you discover your new life.

Exercise Two: Tell the Story of Your Life

Write a story describing a day in your ideal life. Start with, "Once there was a thirty-six-year-old woman who lived in Chicago. She was a producer for an award-winning news program. Every day she . . ."

"Once there was a fifty-eight-year-old man who lived on a ranch in Montana with his horses and a fabulous woman who loved him a lot. Each day they rode into the mountains and . . ."

Where do you live? Where do you work? Who else is in your life? Start with the time you wake up, and describe the day in as much detail as possible—right down to what you have for lunch and when you take the dog for a walk. The more clearly you see your castle, the more inspiring your journey to it will be.

Exercise Three: Cast Yourself Against Type

Examine the negative assumptions you've been carrying around about yourself. Trapeze artists have a saying, "Fat Don't Fly." They don't mean body fat, they mean brain fat. "I'm not the salesman type." "I'm not the flirtatious type." "I'm not the type to stand up in front of people and speak." "I'm the shy type." "I'm not the political type." Who made up all that stuff? Did you or did someone else? It doesn't really matter. The important thing is to drop these assumptions if they don't serve you.

You're not a type. You are a living, breathing organism full of stunning surprises and bold actions. So just for fun, do something that is decidedly against your "type." If you are the shy and retiring type, show up at an event you'd typically skip and—as the "gregarious type"—introduce yourself to everyone there. If you are the self-deprecating type, catch yourself whenever you deflect a compliment by putting yourself down. Substitute a gracious, secure, and reaffirming response.

To you: "I thought that was a great presentation last week. I got a lot out of it."

Old response: "Really? I thought I was a little bit off."

New response: "Thanks, that means a lot to me."

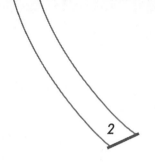

2

THE MAKING
OF A COACH

"Life is either a daring adventure or it's nothing."
—*Helen Keller*

"Life is a banquet and most of us, poor sons of
bitches, are starving to death."
—*Mame in* Auntie Mame

I HAD BARELY SLEPT A WINK at the Detroit hotel where my parents and I stayed the night before the Olympic qualifying trials. For the past several months, I had consistently placed in the top ten in the Amateur Athletic Union meets for the 100-meter freestyle, so my coach thought I had a pretty good shot at qualifying for the American swim team. Now, we were down to the last twenty candidates, and after four years of pulling out all the stops and one long sleepless night, I was feeling anxious because I was tired. And I was feeling tired because I was anxious.

It wasn't just the physical fatigue, in the end, but the mental strain of *anticipating* being worn out in the water that got to me. At fourteen, I hadn't yet learned that it is possible to make a *decision* to draw energy from the task ahead as opposed to being drained by it. The girl looming beside me on the next starting block had big bulging shoulders and big bulging thighs and a fearsome crawl, which I knew because I'd swum against her in previous events, and I wasn't eager to do so again—particularly when I wasn't feeling at the top of my game.

One hundred meters is just two laps in an Olympic pool. That doesn't give you much time to get into the groove if you haven't already found it by the time you hit the water. There are moments in every athlete's life when you get into your groove and stay there for the entire event. When you pull your personal best out of yourself. When you feel free and easy and fluid and strong right up to the finish line. Let's just say, this was not one of those moments. When I touched the pool's side on my return lap, I knew who had won and who had lost: the big girl in the next lane with the shoulders and the thighs had taken the qualifying heat. She was now all that much closer to her goal of getting a shot at the gold. I, on the other hand, was out of the race. I had lost the heat by three quarters of a second, give or take a heartbeat or two.

What happened next was surprising. After feeling a sharp pang of disappointment, the sting of defeat instantly faded away and was followed by a wave of relief. The prospect of living a life that didn't involve spending my evenings and weekends in a cold chlorinated pool beckoned seductively to a girl not yet turned fifteen. Turning myself into one of those fresh, pretty girls who sits in the stands, clapping and cheering and laughing all the way through the race, looked awfully inviting to me as a vision of the future. The girl with the permanently wet hair and the ugly tank suit who never did much of anything but swim and study was history.

My father had taught my brother and me to swim in Lake Erie, which was conveniently located right behind our house in suburban Bay Village. The fact that the smallest of the Great Lakes was polluted and full of dead fish never fazed us, and today, knowing what I know now about environmental toxicity, I'm a bit surprised we didn't all end up sprouting three heads.

At ten, I went away to camp in Farwell, Vermont, and on a lark, entered the Vermont State Swimming Championship in Montpelier. Despite the fact that I didn't even know how to do a racing dive, I did pretty well, and the camp swim coach decided I had what it took to become a real racer. After I got home, my father took me downtown to the Cleveland Athletic Club to meet Bob Busby, the coach of the Coca-Cola Swim Team, one of the best amateur swim programs in the country. I can vividly recall the smell of chlorine and the long dusty beams of sunlight that fell on the pool from the big windows set high in a cavernous ceiling.

"Gail, why don't you get in the water and swim to the other end of the pool, freestyle?" Coach Busby said.

After I'd done that, he said, "Okay, why don't you do the same thing with the backstroke?"

After I'd done that, it was the same thing with the breaststroke and butterfly.

When I was done, he leaned over the edge of the pool and asked, "How would you like to join the team?"

"I would like to very much," I replied, without thinking all that much about it.

I'd like to stop here for just a second to mention that sometimes it's a good idea not to think too much about some things. Sometimes it's just a good idea to get out and *do* it. If I had sat down and thought long and hard about all the hard work involved, the long sleepless nights, the tiring trips, the cold winter evenings when I'd emerge from the pool half-blind from the chlorine with soaking wet hair to wolf down a quick dinner with my mother at Clark's restaurant before heading home, I'd have probably said to hell with it. Which would have been my loss, because swimming taught me some things I don't think I would have learned anywhere else—including how to be a good coach.

Bob Busby was my first professional coach. His low-key, laid-back style has stayed with me as a role model of kind, supportive reinforcement. Busby's philosophy—always an unspoken philosophy, because he was truly the taciturn type—was to be relentlessly positive, regardless of circumstance. He combined a warm personal style with high expectations, lightly and gently applied. Whenever I pulled out all the stops, whenever I put in my personal best, he knew it. But being a laid-back sort of guy, he wouldn't stand up and shout or cheer. You could just hear the note of approval in his voice: "Great. Now I want you to walk around a little bit and loosen up, Gail, and try that again. *Do exactly the same thing, only just a little bit faster.*"

This issue of positive reinforcement in coaching is important, whether we're talking about sports coaching or executive coaching, because a large number of high-profile and successful coaches in a variety of fields take the opposite tack. They go in for what you might call the marine boot camp philosophy, which is to break every player down into tiny little pieces, so that they can put you back together according to a pattern imposed by the coach, as a member of that coach's team. Coaching by negative reinforcement, by saying you are just the worst piece of dirt and I'm ashamed of you for even being here, is an intrinsic part of that philosophy. It's about eliminating the person you were and replacing him or her with a new self molded by the all-controlling master. Coaching by positive reinforcement also creates a new persona, but that new self is not a mechanical robot, a creature molded by the coach; it's the real person already there inside you, inside all of us, waiting to be liberated from its cage by the magic of coaching.

My personal method of coaching is derived from the School of Michelangelo, by which I mean that it is based on removing layers of extraneous material to reveal the fully realized person beneath. Michelangelo spent three years working on his sculpture *David* beneath a temporary shelter set up in the courtyard of the Opera del Duomo in Florence. One of the things that makes the sculpture distinctive, art connoisseurs say, is that he worked from a tall but narrow block of flawed Carrera marble that had been carved and worked on by other sculptors before being abandoned as too messed up to be workable. After Michelangelo finished *David* in 1504 at the age of twenty-nine, the monumental figure was carted through Florence on a four-day procession to a display site in front of the Palazzo Vecchio, where it remained for several centuries. In recent years, the original was replaced by a good marble copy, while the original was moved into a museum to protect it from the elements.

Michelangelo's procedure was to cut the block as if making a deep relief, then to free the three-dimensional figure from its cage of stone. When Michelangelo was done, a Florentine notable asked him how he could possibly have sculpted something so beautiful out of such a rough and flawed block of rock. "David was already there in the marble," he replied. "I just took away everything that was *not* David."

Fritz Kraemer, a prominent international lawyer and a refugee from Nazi Germany, discovered something similar at Camp Claiborne in Louisiana when he encountered the young Henry Kissinger, a private and a fellow refugee. Kraemer took Kissinger under his wing and had him promoted and assigned as a staff officer at headquarters. He then encouraged Kissinger to attend Harvard and study international relations. But whenever he heard himself described as the "discoverer of Henry Kissinger," Kraemer would shout, "My role was not discovering Henry Kissinger. My role was getting Kissinger to discover himself!"

That, in essence, is the role of the coach and the motivator, whether in sports or work or life. A great coach takes away everything that hinders the true person from escaping his block of stone. One very effective way of stripping away those extraneous layers, of liberating your own true form from its emotional and psychological block, is to get out there and enter the arena. And for many of us—because inertia is such a powerful force, because self-doubt can be so crippling, because it's so incredibly easy to say "Oh what the heck, why bother"—we need a coach to motivate us to move and to change.

My first coach was my father, who too had been a competitive athlete in his time and in high school had earned the rare distinction of beating his fellow Cleveland track star Jesse Owens in the 20-yard low hurdles. My father was such a gifted natural athlete that he not only nearly qualified for the Olympics as a runner and hurdle jumper, he also competed in pole-vaulting and discus-throwing. But if my father gave a hoot about not making it to Berlin by a hair, we never heard about it. What we heard, instead, was the value of getting out there and laying yourself on the line. One of my father's heroes was Teddy Roosevelt, a man who embodies just about everything we're trying to honor in this book: passion, purpose, and the compulsion to change. Roosevelt was born with chronic asthma, and with his weak lungs and sickly pallor, he could easily have become a passive and retiring type. Born to great privilege, he might have become indolent and lazy, but he never permitted wealth to rule his life and he bucked every trend like a bronco. He infuriated members of his own class by coming out as a people's man. In a speech he gave at the Sorbonne in Paris in 1910, he challenged his audience to get off the couch and get out into the ring, to fight for what they stood for, to stand up for what they believed in, to never permit themselves to remain passive in the face of uncertainty and insecurity, but above all, to *act*.

It is not the critic who counts—not the man who points out how the strong man stumbles or where the doer of deeds could have done them better. The credit belongs to the man who is actually in the arena; whose face is marred by dust and sweat and blood; who strives valiantly; who errs and comes up short again and again . . . who knows the great enthusiasms, the great devotions; who spends himself in a worthy cause; . . . and who, . . . if he fails, at least, fails while daring greatly. . . .

At Nike, they said the same thing, only shorter:
"Just do it."

I am descended from a long line of motivational speakers and strippers, and if you think the two activities are in any way incompatible, think again. I've come to believe that motivational coaching and stripping are really two sides of the same coin. Both disciplines specialize in getting people to reveal themselves to an audience, as well as to themselves. My father's third cousin on his mother's side was William Jennings Bryan (1860–1925), a two-term congressman from Nebraska, a three-time presidential candidate, the Secretary of State under President Woodrow Wilson, and the greatest orator and motivational speaker of his time. My father's third cousin on his father's side was the equally memorable Gypsy Rose Lee (1914–1970), who referred to herself not as a stripper but as an "ecdysiast"—or "striptease artist."

Gypsy's real name was Rose Louise Hovick, and she got her start on the stage with her younger sister, June, starring in a vaudeville review called "Madame Rose's Dancing Daughters," Madame Rose being their mother and founding ecdysiast of the clan. After June gained fame in Hollywood as the actress June Havoc, Rose Louise reinvented herself as an "intellectual stripper" and gave herself the name Gypsy Rose Lee. In 1937—

the year after her third cousin, my father, missed going to Berlin—New York Mayor Fiorello LaGuardia closed down Minsky's Burlesque Theater off Broadway, and Gypsy followed her sister to Hollywood, where she became a big movie star without ever having to take off more than her hat.

Given my family background, it's probably not so surprising that I would grow up to become a motivational speaker and coach who specializes in getting people to reveal themselves to the world in all their power and glory. I am tempted to say *naked* glory, but this is not going to be one of those books. The revelations I help people pull off are not the physical but the psychological and emotional kind. Which—if you are inclined to agree with Henry Kissinger that power is the best aphrodisiac—can be just as sexy and alluring as the other variety.

What I do when I'm doing my personal best as a coach is to motivate people to *step into their power*. In a variety of ways, I've been doing that for people—as well as for myself—all my life. The power I am speaking about is a special form of strength that we already hold deep inside us, but which we often don't know exists; it takes a crisis, or a moment of peril, for us to find it. You've probably heard stories like the one about the woman who lifted the end of a truck in one hand as it was about to crush her baby boy. That's precisely the sort of power I'm talking about, the sort of power that lies latent inside all of us, until— sometimes in a split second—we are called upon to summon it up, and magically and mysteriously, it comes to our aid.

What my work—and this book—is about is helping people to find ways to summon up that special motivating power on a continuous basis, when we are not in a crisis, when the bomb is not about to go off or the truck about to fall on our child. It's about using that power as a propeller, to lift us to extraordinary heights. It's about finding that power to reinvent ourselves as more purposeful, passionate, and effective people. The kind of people who live every moment as if it is full of potential—as T. S. Eliot wrote in "The Love Song of J. Alfred Prufrock": "Should I, after tea and cakes and ices, / Have the strength to force the moment to its crisis?"

In the end, it's really all about passion. It's passion that gives us the energy to go forward when everyone else is falling behind. It's passion that gives us purpose and provides us with the capacity to keep going when any reasonable person would stop. It's passion that is the driver of profits and breakthroughs in business. It's passion that is also the ultimate driver of people. And it's passion that is the source of all of our power and the provider of all of our promise and possibility.

In a world lacking job security, personal security, financial security, or national security, it's passion that sends us out into the world, into the great insecure unknown. I honestly don't know anyone who isn't in some sense between trapezes these days, because disequilibrium is our new normal state. So the real challenge becomes learning to revel in change instead of hunkering down to defend yourself from it.

The main thing about being between trapezes is that you can't hold on to two trapezes at the same time. You have to be willing to let go of the first one and soar through the air before you can even *see* the second, let alone grab it and *swing*. And if it sometimes takes a crisis to find out who you really are in a crunch, sometimes you just need a good coach.

So what holds us back? What keeps us from becoming our own Teddy Roosevelt, our own Florence Nightingale, our own Willy Mays, Jesse Owens, Oprah Winfrey? What keeps us from getting down in the arena, with the blood and the sand and the guts, like Russell Crowe in *Gladiator*?

Some of us are waiting to see how it all works out. We're convinced that our lives are outside our control anyway and that, yes, life *is* a movie that we're sitting back in our seats watching, passively munching on popcorn. While we wait for the next scene to unfold, we pretend that we're not writing the scenes ourselves, or that we're not the heroes in our own dramas, but merely bit players, like Rosenkrantz and Guildenstern in *Hamlet*. While life passes us by, we wait for someone else to buy us tickets to the show.

Some of us are waiting for someone else to give us permission to move forward. For someone in authority to let us know that it's okay to take that next step. Some of us are waiting until we lose weight. Some us are waiting for the planets to be in alignment. Some of are waiting for courage to come to them, as if it needed an engraved invitation. When I was on Oprah's show, one woman in the audience told me that she was planning to write a book.

"That's great," I said. "When?"

"I'm waiting for the courage," she said.

As I told her, here's the good news about courage: *It comes with action.* It doesn't come waltzing up to our doorstep, all gift wrapped and neatly tied up in a bow. It does come, the moment we step forward, the moment we step up to the plate. We think that because we can't see the trapeze through the mist and the fog that it isn't there. We know all our options, right?

Wrong.

As Charles Darwin once said, "It's not the strongest species that survives, it's not even the most intelligent, it is the one most responsive to change." This is about letting go of our predetermined options. This is about thinking more broadly and more boldly about the next stage in our lives. So many times when we think that way, we get smacked in the face by what we are told is reality. How many plans and heart-stopping successes have been squelched by those two words, "Get real"? Getting real is about denying the magic and wonder of life. It's about settling for other people's reality instead of creating one of our own.

Many of us won't take the step out into the arena because we refuse to let go of the past—those paralyzing assumptions about our lives and our limitations that tell us, like the voice of evil in a medieval morality play that whispers over your shoulder, "You'll never have enough money. You'll never have enough time. You'll never have enough love. You'll never get married. You'll never follow your dream."

It's like the Rolling Stones song "Am I tough enough?" "Am I rich enough?" "Am I young enough?" "Am I smart enough?" "Thin enough?"

The answer to all those questions is *yes*. You are tough enough, rich enough, young enough, tall enough. (We *all* know we're not thin enough.) One woman told me that she was planning to become a lawyer, but that when she told her husband she was going to law school, he said, "What, are you nuts? Do you know how old you'll be when you graduate? You'll be fifty!"

To which she replied, "Well, I'll be fifty anyway."

Some of us are waiting for more information, more data, more pie charts. *I'm just waiting for one more pie chart before making my move out of the stands and into the field.* Let's think for a moment about the fact that while there is an obesity epidemic raging in the United States, the best-selling book genre is the diet book. Most of us would agree that most of the books are pretty similar. It's not a lack of *information* that makes people not lose weight. It's a lack of *motivation*. It's about having a vision of what "good" would look like. It's about enabling yourself, in the end, to step into your power.

Some of us are waiting because it's more important for us to be right about all the things that are wrong with the world before we take our first giant step. We're seeing the opposite bar swinging in and swinging out, and each time it comes toward us, we think we'll wait for the next one because it'll be somehow better. We're like the character in the Woody Allen story who says that since the universe is due to implode in four hundred million years, what's the point of doing anything now?

MY FIRST MENTOR

My first job was with a great coach. Bud Wilkinson had been the legendary coach of the championship football team the Oklahoma Sooners. He had recently retired from coaching full-time to take a position as head of the Washington, D.C.–based Lifetime Sports Foundation, a nonprofit motivational institute funded by the AMF/Brunswick sporting goods company. The foundation's mandate was to keep the public interested in sports for their entire lives, not just in high school and college, and since the sponsoring company made equipment for golf, tennis, and bowling, those were the sports it was possible to stick with your entire life.

Needless to say, Bud Wilkinson and I clicked on the spot, and I was hired on the spot. Wilkinson was the quintessential coach and motivator, and he reminded me instantly of my father—the same verve, the same dynamism, the same insatiable get up and go. He took me under his wing, and because he had to give motivational speeches all the time, I got to be pretty good at writing them. Wilkinson was also on the President's Council on Physical Fitness and Sports and was truly the embodiment of a man who had stepped fully into his power. He was tall, well-built, intensely charismatic, and just radiated all of the reasons that he was such a powerfully motivated and motivating guy. Players loved playing for him, and he loved his players. He was a big believer in the positive reinforcement school of coaching, and his point of view was, you're *already* terrific, it's just a matter of being motivated to bring out your own greatness, in your own way, and at your own pace.

After moving to New York a year later, I was fortunate to land a job with Channel 2 news, the CBS affiliate. Tom Swofford, the wonderful man I had interviewed with, called me two weeks after our meeting, precisely as he had promised. He had good news.

"I've got something for you."

And he had bad news.

"You are the new manager of the Channel 2 film library!"

This was not really bad news, but I have to admit I swallowed hard, because I hadn't the faintest idea about running a library, and librarians had always frightened me. I immediately called Bud Wilkinson and asked for his advice.

"Gail," he said, "you will never know everything about everything, but there is always someone out there who knows everything about something. What you do know how to do is find that expert, and you do know enough to ask the right questions so that you can learn from her or him."

I did exactly that. I called the director of the New York Film Library and made an appointment with him, during which I explained my predicament. On his lunch hour on my first day at work, he came over and walked me through what I needed to do. Every lunch for the following week, he would stop by to help me reorganize the WCBS TV film library. At the end of the week, I signed my paycheck for $150 over to him, and I didn't have to twist his arm very hard to take it. That was the first time I ever hired a consultant.

My next stop was player promotion for the New York Yankees, then owned by CBS. The mandate was to get players to visit schools and to get groups of people to the stadium. Since the Yankees were in last place when I joined up, there was ample room for improvement. For even the weekend games, the sea of empty seats could be a little discouraging. We did have Yankee hostesses in Bill Blass uniforms, with white felt fedoras—very stylish and classy.

The part of the job that I liked best was that it gave me an opportunity to do a little coaching on the side. I was the only woman to have a front office job with the team, and I became the players' sounding board, part shrink, part den mother—although I was probably more like a den sister. Players would plop themselves down in my office and let it all hang out. From time to time, I was able to say something helpful.

Once Joe Pepitone, the Yankees' top hitter after Mickey Mantle, came in and sat down in my office and, opening up a paper bag, pulled out a great big hot pastrami sandwich on rye with pickles. He sat in my office grunting and eating for a while before he finally revealed what was bothering him. He had struck out the last five or six times he'd stepped up to the plate, and he was worried about falling into a serious slump.

"You know," I said, after pondering his predicament for a moment or two, "it's a funny thing, because I was just thinking what a great job you've got—every time you step up to the plate, it's a whole new beginning. There's no carry over. It really doesn't matter what happened last time, or the time before that, because it doesn't affect you in any way. Every 'at bat' is like a rebirth."

He stood up and smiled and that afternoon, I was sitting in my usual seat in the front row right by the plate when Joe Pepitone got up to bat. On the first pitch, he hit a home run, and after he rounded the bases and came home, he saw me waving and flashed me a little thumbs-up.

AVON

My next job was with the San Francisco–based advertising agency Allen & Dorward, the New York office of which handled one major account: the National Football League. The NFL's big public promotion in those days was a program called the NFL Training Table Food Program, which dispensed nutritional education and advice. Allen & Dorward would line up the sponsors, and we would create events where we'd invite food editors to breakfasts or luncheons at elaborate venues like the St. Regis Hotel.

I had been at Allen & Dorward for only a few months when an executive recruiter who shared office space with the agency came up to me and said, out of the blue, "I'd like to send you out on an interview with Avon."

"Why on earth should I want to do that?" I asked.

Avon was a superior sort of company, he said, where quite a few of the senior people who'd been there for years were now being very well compensated. I didn't really know much about Avon apart from the fact that it was a cosmetics company that sold products door to door by the direct sales method. I had heard, of course, about Avon ladies, who by then were being referred to as "sales representatives."

I also knew something about direct sales because at the time, my father was president of the Cleveland-based Kirby Vacuum Cleaner Company, which sold vacuum cleaners door to door, using only men as salespeople, on the theory that men could handle the equipment and be most effective in dealing with "housewives," as they were then known.

When I told my father that I was talking to Avon, he told me that Avon was about as good as it got when it came to direct selling. Direct selling was of course easy to dismiss because the (often erroneous) image was that the people who did it, whether they sold cosmetics or vacuum cleaners or Fuller Brushes, were often people who did not have a lot of other options in life. In fact, a running joke at Avon about the representatives was, "If they can fog a mirror, recruit them."

What my father saw was not a lot of losers, but people who could be *motivated* to achieve miracles. Every once in a while, I used to attend one of my father's motivational speeches when I was in town. They were absolutely riveting. He would tell his people—because they truly were *his* people—how much he believed in them, and that armed with his abiding faith in them, they should have faith in themselves. Rather than snobbishly dismissing direct selling as a last-ditch fall-back, my father saw direct selling as providing people "without a lot of other options in life" with an incredible opportunity to become all that they wanted to be, as the army recruiting slogan put it.

The greatest thing about direct selling, my father told me, is that you don't need a college degree or special talent or good looks or the right accent to succeed. You just needed to want to do it badly enough, and it could transform your life. In his speeches to his sales force, he always emphasized that there were no limits to what you could do or what you could become if you were powerfully motivated. And he would tell his people that this particular company was the best possible partner they could have to become the person they'd always wanted to be.

I ended up going on seven interviews at Avon, each one more

frustrating than the last. They obviously didn't really know who or what they were looking for. My last interview was with a big tall southern good old boy by the name of Ed Carter, who finally said, in that deep southern drawl of his, "So Gail, *whah* do you want to work at Avon?"

"I don't know that I *do* want to work at Avon," I burst out, in frustration. "I don't even know what the job *is*. Because nobody seems able or willing to tell me what the job is. If you can tell me what it is, great. Otherwise, I think we're all wasting our time."

That must have done it because I was given an offer a couple of days later. I became Avon's first female marketing planner, a position that I was initially informed would pay the then-whopping salary of twenty-five thousand dollars in 1974. When human resources offered me nineteen thousand, five hundred dollars, I was insulted and wasn't shy about saying so. I'll never forget the response I got, which would be illegal today.

"What's the big deal? You're married, aren't you? Doesn't your husband have a good job?"

When I went to my boss for the first time to ask for a raise, he told me flat out, "Gail, we don't pay women any more than you're making."

This was the same guy who, after finding out that I was recently married, said without hesitation, "Gail, you aren't going to run off and have a baby, are you?"

"Well," I replied, "now that you mention it, as a matter of fact, I am."

The day I joined Avon they moved into their new building at 9 West 57th Street. The place was stunningly elegant, with breathtaking views of Central Park, and it made a startling statement about what kind of company it was—and what they aspired to be. The space itself was motivational and inspirational. As a marketing planner in the incentives department, my job involved motivating the sales force, which was a complex numbers-driven, equation-driven process, involving nearly three thousand district managers who managed some five hundred thousand sales representatives all across the country.

The key to my job was motivating the district managers to motivate their representatives. And the basic way to do that was to provide a new and, we hoped, alluring package of incentives tied to every two-week sales campaign. To get a feel for what the Avon representatives did, I went door to door with a number of them as a kind of orientation. I can remember being pregnant with Kate and wandering door to door in the Bronx with a woman who had dedicated her life to selling for Avon. I was knocked out by the whole-hearted commitment to the company that these women exhibited and would often wonder if the richly compensated men in the front office truly appreciated what these women were doing for them, out on the streets, pounding the pavement, every day of their working lives.

After my more formal orientation, I wrote a report and presented it to the head of the sales department with all sorts of suggestions that I thought might be good ideas for improving the performance of the organization. Good idea? No, bad idea. My boss's attitude shocked me. He was personally insulted.

"I've got to believe," he said through gritted teeth, "that we must have been doing something right for ninety years."

I felt totally deflated.

For my first fragrance launch of a new perfume called Odyssey a year later, we needed to create a new package of incentives. For this particular launch, it was going to be a nightgown and robe combination, and the moment I saw the sample, I absolutely hated it. The people responsible for preparing the sample were shocked.

"Look, Gail," they said, "it isn't about what *you* like, it's about what *they* like."

The implicit suggestion, of course, being that these women in Oshkosh, Wisconsin, or Dubuque, Iowa, had very poor taste, and this standard stuff was good enough for them. I didn't think so. Hoping to confirm my basic instincts, I called up Florence Skelly, a senior partner at the esteemed market research firm Yankelovich, Skelly and White.

"What you want to give them," she said, "is something they would want to have if they had more money. Don't give them what they already have, but what they dream about having."

Bud Wilkinson and my father had all always said that whenever in doubt, follow your instincts. My instincts told me that I had to do this one differently. Focus groups will tell you what people think they like, but they won't tell you what they really want. My instincts told me that raising the bar, certainly when it comes to trying to motivate and inspire people to perform, is always a more effective approach than lowering the bar. In a way, it was all part of asking myself that all-important question, "How good can we make it?" Making the assumption about the human spirit that "Oh, it's good enough" just isn't good enough.

After giving myself permission to go out on a limb, the sales of Odyssey skyrocketed. Credit went not only to the quality of the fragrance but also to the quality of the incentives. Needless to say, I was thrilled. Then, shortly after that, after six months on the job, I was crushed. My six-month review came back from HR, and it said that while my creativity was off the charts, that operations thing was a problem. To my boss, who spent more than three hours elaborating over every single flaw he could unearth, I asked, "Do you think I should leave Avon?"

"I'm not suggesting that you leave Avon," he said, a little flabbergasted at my response to what he regarded as sensible criticism. "I am suggesting that you improve in these areas."

"Oh," I said.

What I later realized was that this was yet another example of the boot camp school of coaching and motivation. Motivating you by knocking you down and knocking you down again until you pick yourself up off the floor and are determined to do better, even if it kills you.

We had a program called the President's Club, which was comprised of the top 10 to 15 percent of Avon representatives, based on annual sales volume. There wasn't a whole lot of turnover in this group, because 10 to 20 percent of the sales force routinely produced 40 percent of the sales. They asked me to create an incentive program to honor them, and we came up with the President's Celebration, which was our way of letting these wonderful people know just how good we thought they already were. Up until then, the program had always been referred to as a Challenge, placing the emphasis on all the stuff you would have to do to be admitted to the elite club. I deliberately changed that to Celebration, because we wanted the message to be: *You are already good, and we know that.*

It was a huge event, and I had to put together a detailed plan and present it to the president of Avon and other senior executives in the boardroom. Each person at the meeting was supposed to get a presentation deck, made up of pieces of paper with basic points on it with bullets, a kind of precursor to a Power Point presentation. I started my big presentation, providing the background, the opportunity, and the concept. I was about half way through my talk when I realized that I'd forgotten to hand out the presentation deck, but I kept going, figuring there was no reason to break the rhythm by passing them out. My boss, and almost everyone, save for the head of sales promotion, who wasn't crazy about it, loved the presentation. When I was done my boss said to me, in private, "Well, that was an interesting strategy."

"What strategy?"

"Leaving out the presentation deck. It made us focus more on you."

"Oh, *that* strategy."

My next stroke of good luck was sitting next to a man named Bob Breen on a flight to a sales conference. "What would you really like to do around here?" he asked.

"I want to work in the conference department," I replied unhesitatingly.

The conference department produced events that were the equivalent of full-scale theatrical productions, with special effects, original music, and live casts. Not long after that, Bob Breen was made director of the conference department, and he hired me to come work for him.

The conferences were big motivational events, typically held in a hotel ballroom in the center of the largest town or city in the region. They were multimedia extravaganzas put together to motivate district managers to create breakthrough sales in the critical fourth quarter. Bob knew I had a background in theater. Thinking about these events, I thought about Aristotle and about the fact that every event had to have a beginning, a middle, and an end, like a play. Every action had to have motivation, so that when it happened, it struck the audience as a natural flow from the action preceding it. My title was manager of conferences, and we would produce every one like a Broadway show, with original music, lyrics, script, and choreography.

The basic theme was always the same, always celebratory.

"You are *already* so great" was the subtext of everything that we did and everything that we said. We made the higher-ups the heroes of our dramas, but also celebrated the representatives and district managers, the backbone of the company. Taking a page out of my father's book, the basic theme always was that the only limitation you had was the size of your dream.

District managers were the most critical and influential segment of the sales force. They were responsible for recruiting, training, and motivating Avon representatives, and there wasn't anything that we wouldn't do for them. We'd fly them to Paris, Hawaii, provide every little elegant touch, every bit of music and song. There was no big thing and no small thing we wouldn't do. In many cases, their husbands couldn't keep up with them. There was a high divorce rate among district managers, and an even higher divorce rate among regional managers, in part because many were more motivated and were gaining more recognition at work than their husbands. We kept trying to work with them to get their husbands on our side. We were often fighting a losing battle, because the more we celebrated their wives, the more effectively we motivated them to succeed, the more they felt, "Well, she's such hot stuff now, so where does that leave me?"

In 1986, Avon turned one hundred, and it was a great celebration. But not long afterward, panic set in. Under CEO Hicks Waldron, diversification had become the name of the game. Waldron had come out of the wine and spirits industry, had been a member of Avon's board of directors, and had been brought in to accomplish a radical shift of strategic direction. And he did, to his credit, introduce strategic planning into the mix of management styles at Avon. Under the mantra of diversification, and at the behest of big-name consultants, the company made an enormous investment—or gamble—in home health care, which was considered to be a growth industry. The logic of the move was perfectly sound. It wasn't that it wasn't a good idea. But for a number of reasons, having mainly to do with poor execution and faulty timing, the effort fell flat on its face.

The net result was that because home health care exerted an enormous drag on our earnings, we went from being a cash-rich to a cash-poor company, and our faltering numbers began to send our stock through the floor. Suddenly our one-hundred-year-old company, which had for much of its existence been the pride of its industry and a business model worth emulating, had become a takeover target. What was even more insulting was that the people trying to take us over were the upstart Mary Kay cosmetics.

We ended up having to fight our way out of this big mess, and I have to say, I loved every minute of it. Whenever I say that sometimes it takes a crisis to find out who you are as a person, a country, or a company, I think about Avon undergoing its wrenching transformation in the late eighties, which I had the *privilege* not only to live through, but help guide. You can buy the company, we said to ourselves, but you can't buy the people, or our attitude. Despite the fact that in objective terms things were very difficult, personally I was thrilled by the rich smell of change in the air.

But when things are going along just fine, that's when inertia sets in. Nobody wants to change, nobody has an incentive to change, when things are just hunky-dory. But in a crisis, people start to listen to each other, as opposed to just hearing themselves talk. In a crisis, people start to take the idea of reinvention seriously. We had to reinvent the company, or somebody else was going to do it for us. Since my stint as director of conferences, I had been promoted to a number of interim positions, then to vice president of public affairs in 1982. In such a role, I helped guide the company through this painful yet exhilarating transition. And our new focus was to become the company that, as our mission statement put it, best understood and served the product, service, and self-fulfillment needs of women globally.

By 1986, as we celebrated our centennial, our district managers were telling us that women weren't staying at home any more and that we had to follow our customers into the work place. But in management, way up in our fancy white offices on West 57th Street, we didn't hear it. We kept telling them that they had to try harder. We had failed to understand that we had to sell to women in a setting where it was convenient for them to buy, not convenient for us to sell. There was a Darwinian evolution under way in society, and we were failing to respond to a massive environmental shift that was comparable to global warming.

Until we nearly went under, we neither knew nor cared about the changing environment. Typically, we wait and see what the weather may bring. I kept trying to say, "How good could we make this?"

And in response, I kept hearing what I'd heard ten years before from my first boss in response to my suggestions for change: "We've got to have been doing something right for ninety years." Now, we had the evidence that while that might have been true at one time, it simply wasn't true now. We had to galvanize ourselves into becoming a different company. We were on the edge, nearly flat on our backs, and I have to say, it was dramatic. Just as I do now with everyone I speak to at a motivational event, or with one of my private players, we had to figure out how to take the passion and the energy that we were able to muster during those times of crisis and apply it to our daily lives.

This was the crisis that defined us as a company. This was the crisis, that in a way, we had all been waiting for. This was the crisis in which we had to reinvent ourselves before someone else did. Of all my fabulous times at Avon, this was my favorite. When you're up against the wall or down on one knee, when you're about to be taken over in life, or in a company, or in a family, or even in a country, that's when you figure out who you really are, what you stand for, and who you could be.

A key part of our strategic reorientation was to enhance the image of Avon among more educated and affluent women. In 1987, we conceived of a program called the Women of Enterprise Awards, in partnership with the United States Small Business Administration. We would present awards annually at a magnificently produced event held at New York's Waldorf-Astoria hotel, to a group of women entrepreneurs who had achieved outstanding business success, often overcoming tremendous odds and adversity to do so—either economic or personal, or both.

Every year, we would read hundreds of applications from women across the country who had started businesses and persevered and ultimately prevailed. One of our awardees in 1989 was Carolyn Stradley, who overcame almost insurmountable odds to found C & S Paving, a general contracting company in Georgia whose annual revenues quickly exceeded two and a half million dollars. Carolyn's mother had died when she was eleven, and she and her brothers found themselves effectively orphaned when their father disappeared and left the kids to fend for themselves. She temporarily escaped from her dreadful life when she married her high school sweetheart at fifteen, who died five years later of a heart attack, leaving Carolyn once again alone. She worked for a construction company for three years after her husband's death, until she founded C & S Paving in 1976. In 1985, the firm won the contract for a major project at Dobbins Air Force Base, the largest United States Air Force contract ever awarded to a woman-owned business.

Walking out of one of those events at the Waldorf one afternoon, with tears in my eyes—there was never a dry eye in the house when those women's life stories had been told—I thought to myself, "Well, these women overcame tremendous adversity to establish these companies, all because they had a vision of the future and followed it to the end of the rainbow." Standing on the sidewalk outside the Waldorf, waiting for a cab, I began to think, "What about the rest of us? Even if we weren't facing crisis, or adversity, couldn't we still do great things and prevail?" The real epiphany for me was thinking that if these women, who had everything going against them, could do it, why couldn't I, who had everything going *for* me. Because this wasn't really about starting a business. It was about creating a life.

LIFEDESIGNS

In March 1995, I created a new division for Avon called Lifedesigns, whose mission was to persuade women not only that they could be beautiful, but they could create a beautiful life. Our first two-day workshop was held in the company auditorium at 9 West 57th Street. Everything was executed down to the slightest detail—the flowers, the food, even the music was inspiring. The theme of the workshop was "Creating a Life You Can Love." We invited a number of very successful career women to our trial workshop, to be our guests as we worked the kinks out. What we knew about these women was that they had led successful careers. What we surmised was that their lives may have been usurped by those careers. And what we heard, when we listened to what they had to say, was, "Okay, I've got a job. Now what I need is a life."

Go home and throw away fifty things, I told the workshop participants. We don't know what the future holds. We are all *between trapezes*, which was the first time that I had ever used the phrase. As of this moment, you are—we are—ready to let go of the old assumptions, the old concepts, the old rules. We haven't yet reached out and grabbed that new self, that new reality, that new trapeze. This moment is both thrilling and terrifying. We are not holding on to anything at this point. This is a defining moment because we have, paradoxically, renounced all our definitions. We have to let go; we are floating in the universe. Everything is up for grabs. But this is, counterintuitive as it may seem, *one of the best places you could possibly be in your life*. If you're open to all that great stuff out there, waiting in the wings, all that open space, right now everything and anything is possible.

An effective way to get rid of your past, I told the women in the workshop, is to complete it. One woman was divorced, but her marriage wasn't over for her. One of the things she had to do was complete that process. Leaving the workshop, she went to the garage where her car was parked, and as she walked toward her car, she saw her ex-husband walking toward her. "I was going to call you," she said. He said, "That's funny, I was thinking about you a lot today."

The message she took away was that it was no longer necessary to be enemies, and that one of the things she had to release was the animosity that was eating away at her. *She didn't need to be right about what a jerk he had been.*

Letting Go of the Little Things

Little things can eat away at you and hold you back, little things you didn't even know that you had, little things that you carry around with you for years. One woman who came to a workshop said that when she was ten, she had desperately wanted one of those expandable plastic charm bracelets, and that her parents had given one to her cousin for her birthday but never to her. So jealous was she of her cousin that after more than twenty years, she still hadn't forgiven her. She decided that night to call her cousin, and say, "I have never been as open with you as I might have been if this hadn't happened." Another woman who heard this story was busy searching her drawers and closets for things to throw out that night, and wouldn't you know, came across an expandable charm bracelet she'd had since she was a child. Rather than throwing it out, she decided to bring it in the next day. We staged a tenth-birthday party for the woman who'd longed for the bracelet for twenty years and gave it to her with much fanfare. Now that's what you call kismet.

You never know what's going to happen when you let go of something. We think we're supposed to know everything. We have plans, strategies, futures, and very exact ideas of what we are going to do when we get there. We're not trained to be open to kismet, much less believe in it. Or even the unpredictable and the unexpected. It's so magical, and magic can be threatening to our sense of ourselves as rational beings. As a result, we probably miss out on an awful lot of delight in our lives.

After two years of running Lifedesigns as a division of Avon, I took my next swing on the big trapeze and flung myself out into wide open space and became a woman of enterprise myself. A defining moment for me had been when, outside the Waldorf I had asked, "What about the rest of us?" and created Lifedesigns. A second defining moment came when I decided to leap off the diving board and invent the water on the way down. Sometimes, you have to do something because you just can't *not* do it, even when there's no evidence that it's going to work. I acquired Lifedesigns from Avon, and after conducting motivational workshops based on the program for a number of years, I branched out into motivational speaking and executive coaching. As the business has evolved, and after working with a large number of individuals and groups, I've developed a five-step process of personal transformation entitled Between Trapezes: Five Steps to Flying into Your Next Great Life™, which forms the basis for all of my counseling and coaching sessions. Here are those steps.

1. Build the castle first. Imagine exactly what *your* idea of "good" looks like. Fill in every detail, every color. Own that vision. Ask yourself the question, "How good can I make it?"

2. Fat don't fly. Let go of the old trapeze—the old title, the old role, the old view of yourself. Remember that "fat don't fly." Make a list of the ideas, concepts, points of view that no longer serve you. Throw them out.

3. Listen to discover new possibilities, new solutions, new methods of operation, rather than insisting that things fit with what you already know or match *somebody else's* idea of "good."

4. Never confuse falling with failing. The greatest flyers are always the greatest fallers.

5. "Get the bench!" Practice distinguishing between fact and interpretation. Make up interpretations for the things that happen that propel you toward the life of your dreams.

Just as I was able to do in my own life and bring the experiences I gathered to my workshops and my coaching, in the succeeding chapters, we'll see how a cast of characters—my private "players"—revel in the art of self-reinvention. We'll watch as they undergo a coaching process, the magic of which, in the end, I owe to the wonderful coaches who have coached me over the years, and whose collective wisdom I feel proud and privileged to be able to pass on to you.

The lyrical beauty of these often frightening moments is summed up in a beautiful poem:

Sometimes I feel that my life is a series of trapeze swings.

I'm either hanging on to a trapeze bar swinging along

Or, for a few moments in my life, I'm hurtling across space

In between trapeze bars . . .

The transition zones in our lives are incredibly rich places

They should be honored, even savored.

They are the most alive, most growth-filled,

Most passionate, most expansive moments of our lives.

Because hurtling through the void

We may just learn how to fly.

—*Danaan Parry*

Exercise One: The Michelangelo Method

The essence of good coaching is helping others to remove the artificially constructed barriers that prevent them from realizing their natural greatness. A good player will record and retain the encouraging voice of his coach so that he can replay it at the moment he is asked to beat his old record. A good player stores that positive voice deep inside, where it will continue to resonate, as opposed to dissipate. This is the voice of *David*, asking to be released from his block of marble. Search your memory for those times when someone said something really terrific about you. "You are really good at ____(fill in the blank)." Turn up the volume on those positive voices. Press "Star 3-Delete" on the negative.

Exercise Two: The Bud Wilkinson Method

You will never know everything about everything. But there will always be someone who knows everything about something. When faced with a challenge where you possess no expertise, find the experts and ask their help, support, and advice. Don't listen to those who say, "They're too important and busy to be bothered. They'll never get back to you." Wrong. People love to be asked for their guidance. Give it a try. You may be surprised.

THE CANDIDATE

NEVER IN MY WILDEST DREAMS did I imagine that I would ever coach a candidate running for president. But that is why it pays to follow your wildest dreams, because you never know what life might or might not bring you, and it's a good idea to be ready when things fly at you out of the blue. Whether you're running for president or were recently laid off from a middle management position in computer sales, whether you're a race car driver, a jazz guitarist, or an astronaut, the real test of courage and character is to be able to make that next big jump, that next huge leap of faith, to grasp the trapeze that you have reason to believe is out there waiting for you—even if you can't see it through the mist and the fog. What makes life worth living, I believe, is taking a deep breath and leaping into the void. And in the case of this particular story, my sudden involvement in the center of a presidential campaign was as much of a leap to a new trapeze for me as it was for the candidate.

One day in the summer of 2003, I had a meeting in my New York office with Tom Gibson, the founder and chief executive of a Virginia-based professional services company that, under the brand name IntellEvents, owns and produces a spectacular series of educational events for working women known as Uncommon Women on Common Ground™. These events honor women from around the world who bring a variety of resources to bear on a wide range of problems impacting women, from domestic violence to war on civilians to drug abuse to AIDS. At one of these events, held in Jacksonville, Florida, I was privileged to be a keynote speaker, along with the actress Cicely Tyson and the activist Kerry Kennedy Cuomo. I got to know Tom Gibson a little and found him one of a rare breed—a true kindred spirit.

Tom and I were discussing the possibility of doing a series of events together when he mentioned, in passing, that his schedule was looking a bit tight at the moment. He was producing a number of events for his father-in-law's presidential campaign. By then, I knew that his father-in-law was Senator Bob Graham, the two-term former governor and three-term senior senator from Florida. We immediately began talking about how things were going with the campaign. Though I don't make a habit of watching political events on TV—or didn't then—I had happened to catch Bob Graham's campaign launch on CNN a few weeks before. While it was abundantly clear that Senator

Graham had the strongest possible credentials for the job, it was also clear that his central message wasn't coming through or cutting through the thicket of early-season campaign clutter.

Tom Gibson happens to be an old hand on the motivational/inspirational speaker circuit, and was well aware from personal experience that his father-in-law's delivery and general presentation required both refinement and pizzazz. It may be a sign that I'm not the shy type that I immediately spotted my next trapeze, dangling there rather invitingly—you might even say, seductively.

"You know," I said, musingly, as if the thought had just occurred to me—which in a way, it had—"maybe I ought to be coaching *him*."

"You know what?" Tom immediately replied. "I think that's a *terrific* idea."

Things moved pretty quickly after that. Tom set up a time for me to meet with the senator during his next tip to New York, about ten days thence. That gave me some breathing room to do a little research on the Florida senator because, quite honestly, although I was familiar with the name, I really didn't know that much about him. Curiously, my husband, Jim, a former news director for WCBS News in New York and a self-described political junkie, didn't know all that much about him either. As I later learned, that is, in a way, the quintessential Bob Graham: He is a public servant in the mold of Harry Truman, a man focused on doing what's right and not much given to tooting his own horn.

Tom Gibson asked the senator's campaign coordinators to

send me a video reel of his most recent TV appearances, along with a sheaf of his positions on a variety of policy issues. I also ran a search on the Internet, which turned up any number of fascinating facts about his life. By the time I was done, I knew that the senior senator from Florida was sixty-six years old and that he had been born in Dade County, Florida, the son of Ernest "Cap" Graham, himself a former Florida state senator, mining engineer, dairy/cattleman, real estate developer, and all-around chunk of entrepreneurial dynamite. Bob's mother, Hilda, had been a schoolteacher, which I realized could be an important key to his character, because the offspring of teachers are often good students.

Senator Bob Graham comes, I learned, from a distinguished and accomplished family. Cap Graham founded a dairy at Pennsuco in 1932, which managed to flourish even in the depths of the Depression. The Graham family continues to operate dairy, beef cattle, and pecan farms in Florida and Georgia and is a prominent player in the economy of their home state today. One of Bob's older brothers, Philip, is the former publisher of the *Washington Post* and *Newsweek*. Another older brother, William, is the chairman of The Graham Companies of Miami Lakes, Florida, a real estate development company that Bob and Bill founded together back in 1960 to intelligently plan and develop the community of Miami Lakes. It now boasts a population of more than twenty-two thousand and employs over ten thousand people in its industrial and office parks and commercial centers.

After serving several terms as a representative in the Florida State Legislature, Bob was elected a state senator in 1970, was reelected in 1974, successfully ran for governor in 1978 against long odds, was reelected in 1982, was elected to the United States Senate in 1986, and has since gone on to serve three terms as senator. So what did that tell me about Senator Bob Graham? Well, for one thing, as Senator Graham himself will freely admit, while he might not be Mr. Charisma, he has also never lost an election. Clearly, the people of Florida see greatness in this man, who continues to be the most popular elected official in Florida history.

One of the most interesting things that I learned about Senator Graham was that starting all the way back in 1974, when he was serving in the Florida State Senate, he launched the unique concept of "Workdays," establishing a custom that he religiously followed for the next thirty years. On an average of once a month, Bob Graham takes a day away from his office or home and works at a different job in his home state. Since he began doing it, with remarkably little fanfare, this independently wealthy graduate of Harvard Law School has put in 386 Workdays serving his fellow citizens as a police officer, a railroad engineer, a construction worker, a fisherman, a sanitation man, a factory worker, busboy, a nursing home aide, and a teacher.

On Workday 365, to celebrate the completion of his first year of Workdays, he checked in customers, handled baggage, and helped serve passengers on a US Airways counter at Miami airport. These Workdays, I learned soon enough, are not just some political gimmick. They are a reflection of the seriousness with which Bob takes the role of researcher, learner, and reporter. He has actually taken the knowledge he picked up on those jobs and used it to formulate public policy. Bob, as I have said, is a natural student, a regular knowledge sponge. Whenever he approaches anything, he approaches it as a learning and a growth experience.

Take, for example, the Workday at Florida's Port Manatee in 1997, after which he persuaded President Bill Clinton to establish a federal commission to evaluate crime at our seaports. This concern for security, four years before September 11, made him one of the first U.S. politicians to seriously contemplate the problems facing us with home and port security. What did that tell me about Bob Graham? That he's driven not so much by a desire to speak but by a desire to listen. This is, as you can well imagine, a valuable quality to cultivate, no matter what your goal. As a coach, I work very hard to bring out this quality in every one of the people I work with. Listening, I believe, is the key not just to personal growth, but to leadership. Being a listener means you understand that it's healthy to keep an open mind, and that you don't already know everything—you have to always be learning more. Listening and learning are also the keys to leadership, because they are ongoing processes. Already *knowing* is a static thing; learning is dynamic. Bob Graham is a leader's leader, in that he listens carefully to everything he can possibly pick up about a particular subject, and when he's ready to make up his mind, he does so decisively and with the quiet authority that comes from a wealth of knowledge.

Bob Graham, I learned, represents a new breed of leader: one who listens, learns, is impassioned, decisive, and dedicated; one who is secure to the point of being truly open to discovering new possibilities in himself and the world; one who really will ask— and answer—the question, "How good could we make it?"

I also learned that in the United States Senate—which, as a group, is a pretty intellectually gifted crowd—Bob Graham stands out as an intellect and a scholar. During the 107th Congress in 2001–2002, he served as chairman of the Senate Select Committee on Intelligence. In the wake of the horrific events of September 11, 2001, as chairman he became deeply committed to improving the performance of the nation's intelligence agencies in their responsiveness to the threat of global terrorism. It was during that stint as chairman of that key committee that he first became convinced that his breadth of knowledge and intuitive strengths in this area made making a run for the presidency a compelling life option for him. No one else in that group of candidates, I thought to myself, has anything approaching his track record or credentials. He is politically moderate and un-usually bipartisan, which was why—as one of the articles I read about him flatly stated—a number of the other Democratic can-didates were "trembling" in anticipation of his announcement to run.

The idea of coaching a presidential candidate was clearly a new trapeze for me. I don't imagine you'd be very surprised if I told you that I felt just the least bit intimidated by the task. From the moment I had made my first off-hand commitment to give it a shot, I began to do a little self-coaching. One of the first things I had to do was to remind myself that working with a presidential candidate was probably not all that different from working with a corporate executive, or for that matter, a champion polo player.

I'm still waiting for that polo player.

What all of my coaching is about, in the end, is helping people from all walks of life and with a wide range of goals, skills, and aspirations to learn to step into their own power. As I tell all of my players when they suffer from bouts of self-doubt, there isn't a man or woman in this world who doesn't question their own qualifications and experience and fitness for the task ahead. Whether you are Churchill, Roosevelt, Willy Mays, Oprah, or Maya Angelou, you are going to wonder, from time to time, whether you are really up to the job or the task ahead. Whether that task is finding or quitting a job, or getting married, or catching a prize marlin, a good coach can help you realize that yes, you *can* do it. That yes, damn it, you are *precisely* the right person at the right time. And by the way, don't you forget it!

I don't mind admitting that on the morning of my introductory meeting with the senator I was nervous. To get my mood and my energy up, I deliberately wore my favorite yellow suit. On my way across town I deliberately tried to put a little extra bounce in my step, and I kept telling myself, over and over, "Gail, you're the right person for this engagement. You're going to do what you know how to do."

Of course, I just as easily could have said to myself, "You know, this is crazy. You've never coached a presidential candidate in your life. You have absolutely no track record at this!" The reason I didn't do that was that I've learned to still those voices in my head, which is a form of discipline at least as important as learning any particular skill on earth. I am a big fan of listening, but not to those voices. I was reminded of the schizophrenic mathematician John Nash, played by Russell Crowe in *A Beautiful Mind*, when he responds to the gentleman from the Nobel Prize Committee with whom he sits in the Princeton faculty club, sipping tea. "Do you still . . ." the man asks delicately, his voice trailing off in embarrassment.

"See them?" John Nash asks politely. "Oh yes, I see them, but I choose not to *acknowledge* them. Because like all of our dreams and all of our nightmares, you have to feed them for them to live."

As I was doing everything I possibly could to psyche myself up, a well-dressed and perfectly respectable-looking man walked past me and, turning on a dime, smiled appreciatively.

"You know," he said matter-of-factly, "you look absolutely fabulous."

He said it in a way that was not in the slightest bit sleazy. The only thing I could say was, "Thank you so much," with all the sincerity that I could muster.

That really set me up for the meeting.

I arrived at the conference room in a building a few blocks from my office eager to jump into it. I felt psyched up like a swimmer. Then I was momentarily deflated by the news that the senator was running a little behind schedule. When I later learned that he might be as much as an hour and a half behind schedule, I was shown into the big empty conference room to listen to my own doubting voices, which I was having more and more trouble silencing John Nash–style, with all this time to kill on my hands. My fleeting feelings of inadequacy were scarcely dispelled by the next bit of news: The reason that Senator Graham was late was that he was meeting with the singer Jimmy Buffett, a longtime friend who was committing to some fundraising concerts for the senator's campaign. Well, how about that! Here I was, pacing around in this little airless room like a caged cat, feeling as if the wind was seriously dropping out of my sails by the minute, and all I could conjure up in my mind was an image of Jimmy Buffett, in a flowing Hawaiian shirt, serenading the senator, crooning and plucking away at his guitar while plying him and his staff with the best margaritas that you could possibly imagine straight from the blender. Talk about a tough act to follow!

Then I thought back to my first coach, Bob Busby of Cleveland's Coca-Cola swim team, who would tell us what to do before every swim meet: work on our breathing, loosen up, and remove from our minds all of those doubts that we all have and focus on what we needed to do. What I needed to do at this meeting, I realized, was simple:

- I needed to listen to *him*.

- I needed to make this meeting not about *me*, but about *him*.

- I needed to know what his vision was, and how I could help make it happen.

Another thing that I knew about Bob Graham, without having to do a Google search, was that despite the wealth of differences in our résumés, we both gave speeches for a living. We both are, in a very real sense, live performers. I knew from years of experience that whenever I succeeded in getting an audience to really jump into the palm of my hand, it was when I was my most selfless. Whenever I started worrying about *myself*, I would lose *them*. So the best way not to be nervous was to make this event about him and not about me. Which was all great, except that I knew, sure as shooting, that if he opened the meeting by asking a pointed question like, "How many presidential candidates have you coached before this?" I was toast.

When Senator Graham did finally turn up, he was accompanied by a sizable entourage, which, for some reason, I wasn't expecting. This momentarily threw me off stride, because it felt a little bit more like an inquisition, or even stranger, like inviting the audience in for a private therapy session, than a meet-and-greet job interview. Nevertheless, I was grateful to Tom Gibson for coming to the meeting, because I knew he was a fan and a supporter and that he would be looking to show me in my best light. Just the same, it took a beat or two to get back into my groove. A presidential candidate is the quintessentially public person; there is very little personal privacy in the midst of a political campaign. If I wanted to be a part of this thing, I was just going to have to live with it.

I immediately felt grateful that Florida is in the South, because Bob is the consummate southern gentleman, with lovely manners and a physical grace that make him a much more palpable presence in person than he appears to be on TV. He was immediately gracious, warm, and genuine—not in the slightest bit arrogant, not in the slightest bit taken with himself. I could feel the warmth, the passion, the humor, and the commitment right away. But I also knew that it's easier to feel all that standing five feet away than in a big hall or stadium, much less a televised interview or news conference. In person, they say Al Gore can be extremely warm and personable. Enough said.

If it was true that in many ways he was—as many people had said about him, often admiringly—all substance and no style, all steak and no sizzle, he was nevertheless beautifully dressed, in a well-fitting dark blue suit, nicely set off by an American flag tie, with a commanding physical presence. Judging from photographs, he had lost a good deal of weight. He was looking trim and fit, primed and prepared.

"I've heard so many good things about you from Tom," the senator said, which certainly struck the right note from the start, from my point of view. "It's just such a pleasure to meet you." Then, pleasantries completed and the ice neatly broken, we were off to the races. I already knew what the theme of the meeting would be. It was best put several decades ago by the British novelist E. M. Forster, in *Howard's End*.

> Only connect! Only connect the prose and the passion, and both will be exalted, and human love will be seen at its height. Live in fragments no longer. Only connect, and the beast and the monk, robbed of the isolation that is life to either, will die.

I had hardly had a chance to open my mouth before the senator pulled out a little notebook and began energetically taking down notes, like the eager graduate student he is at heart. It was immediately obvious that, like his Workdays, this was no gimmick. This was the real Bob Graham, and—important for me—a real key to his personality. More than a senator or presidential candidate, Bob was and is at heart an ardent and passionate lover of knowledge. This means that it would be more important for him to learn than to be right, and that it would be more important for him to understand and decide based on that understanding than simply to take the most popular or ideologically determined course.

I began my presentation by saying a few things about stepping into your power. I even got up to show him, in person. I walked out of the room and then back into the room and mimed walking up to a podium with passion, purpose, conviction, and the deep inner knowledge that *you* are the guy, that *you* are already the president, that your castle has already been built and that you are living in it, day in and day out. It's like an actor assuming a part, I said, taking the ultimate leadership position. I talked about how other people have to be able to *feel* that power and that passion.

"Can you say a little more about stepping into your power? What exactly do you mean?" Bob asked very politely, pen poised to take a few additional and clarifying notes.

"It's a mind-set and a practice and a mental discipline," I replied, "not unlike prayer or meditation or yoga. Before every speech, before every presentation, before every big moment in my life, I envision myself stepping into my power. It's like stepping into a suit of clothes. It's the emotional equivalent of a knight, before going into battle, putting on his armor, or the Western rider climbing into his saddle and dusting off his six-shooter. It's inside me. I'm *releasing* it. I'm *exuding* it. If I'm doing it right, I feel it intensely. I believe we all have that power inside us, and that we only have to find ways of tapping it to let it out and transform us into the people we want to be. It's about releasing energy into the universe."

I was just about done.

"You are standing there, Senator, standing in your power. You are allowing it to sweep over you. It's about passion and courage and conviction, and it's also about letting go."

What I didn't say then, but what I want *you* to know, is that you can practice stepping into your own power the next time you walk into a PTA meeting or your next job interview or even a casual conversation with your boss or coworkers. If you immediately have an urge to hide in the corner and feel that you have nothing whatsoever to say, you need to just think to yourself, "What I have to say is worth something, and they will find it interesting." Now that you've stepped into your power, your personal passion, your love of the audience, you can own your own space and fill it with your energy.

That's what we call charisma. It's about stepping into the arena—the arena of life. It's about courage being grounded in action. It's about overcoming that fear that strikes all of us before something big—that maybe *this* is the time we'll really screw up.

Did Bob Graham, who had won every political race in his life, worry that he was not up to the task of winning this, the biggest race of his life? Probably. Why shouldn't he? But just as I was trying to follow my own admonition to make this meeting about him, not about me, I could tell that he was practicing precisely the same discipline. He was making the meeting all about me, not about him. The really great thing was, this hard-edged emotional approach was working wonders for the both of us. We were both listening to each other and on the same wavelength. The feeling was truly electric.

What made it work for me and stilled those doubting voices in my head was the awareness that the senator really was all ears. He was hanging on every word. Like an actor with an audience, a coach needs a good player. Because he was willing and capable of turning himself into a student without worrying about giving up the authority that would have made him the teacher, I immediately knew that I could take risks with him. I immediately knew that he was willing to learn. And that we were going to have fun.

Speaking of fun, I then said a few things about the differences between Bill Clinton and Al Gore. With Clinton, it was all about the *audience* and what he needed to find out from *them*. With Gore, it was all about what *he* knew and how it was his job to teach us, to tell us what he knew. With Gore, the premise was that we needed to know what he knew, because it would be good for us.

"The problem with that approach," I said, "is that we don't *want* to be taught; we want to be *moved*. We don't want a lecture; we want to be *inspired*."

I talked about H. Ross Perot standing up on national TV with those pointy ears and that little pointer and big easel and a white board, pronouncing about the deficit and drawing curves on the board and just boring everybody but the professional economists in the audience to tears. For a compare-and-contrast example, I talked about the presidential candidate Willy Stark in Robert Penn Warren's *All The King's Men*, a thinly fictionalized version of the great populist and longtime governor and senator from Florida's neighboring state of Louisiana, Huey Long, popularly known as "The Kingfish."

I talked about how Willy Stark started out his political career talking about taxes and over time evolved to talking about people's lives. As I spoke, without really thinking about it—because I wasn't thinking, I was performing—I began building my own castle, which was a vision of Bob Graham in the White House and my having been his secret weapon that propelled him there. Curiously enough, I never once thought to myself, "He's behind in the polls. He's not the front runner. He might lose." All that I knew, of course, but in the heat of that moment I forced myself to forget.

I briefly alluded to the fact that he was clearly not the front runner. But I did what I could to turn this liability into an asset. I talked about the championship race horse Seabiscuit coming up from behind and that being small just made him have to run all that much harder. I mentioned the exchange from the movie, when a rival jockey says to Seabiscuit's jockey, "Kinda small, ain't he?" and Seabiscuit's jockey replies, "Yep, and he's going to look a lot smaller in about half a minute." I knew what my job was: to help Bob find within himself the resources to be the man he needed to be to come up from behind and become president. He was going to have to step into the fullness of his power, and I never for one moment doubted that he had it in him to do so.

We cued up the tapes of his most recent TV appearances, and I gave him my two cents, for what it was worth. Being trained as a lawyer, it was immediately apparent that he had a tendency to bury his lead in the body of a dense text, because like a good lawyer, he would gradually build his case to a climactic conclusion, then slowly and deliberately move in for the kill. But in this sound bite world, and under the trying circumstances of a presidential campaign, which is run at least in its initial stages almost entirely off TV appearances and interviews, he needed to think less like a lawyer and more like a journalist. He needed to put that lead paragraph, the paragraph that sums up the story, right up in the front where we can hear it. If Larry King or Tim Matthews or Tim Russert gave him a couple more seconds to add a clause or two, be careful. Stick to making one more key point—not two. And don't, by any means, try to squeeze in another five.

The more cerebral you are, the smarter you are, the harder it can be to be punchy and succinct, because you really enjoy parsing the complexity of it all. The long and the short of it was that because Bob Graham was so smart and so well informed, he was thinking too much and talking too much while he should have been emoting more. The clarity of the message tended to get lost in the flow of the nouns and verbs, and an opportunity for a passionate message to be heard loud and clear was blurred. When it comes to distilling a message, complexity is not a virtue, I insisted. Distilling any substance down to its essence, as we all know, means making it stronger.

In the end, I said, this campaign was not going to be decided by how much you *know*, but by how much you *care*.

I could immediately tell by the look in his eyes that he got it. And I knew I was in. I was literally bouncing back to the office after that first meeting. I had the wonderful feeling that I had nailed it, and all of a sudden, there I was, with the greatest of ease, being a daring young woman on my flying trapeze. Putting together a few notes after the meeting to send him, I stressed a couple of key points:

• People don't *care* what you *know* until they *know* that you *care*.

• You're already the right person, you simply need to reveal it.

During our next phone conversation, I rehearsed a mantra with him that I do with all of my clients, the "From/To" list. These were the attributes that we came up with:

1. From *how much you know* to *how much you care.*

2. From *polishing your image* to *revealing yourself and your passion.*

3. From *controlling* to *letting go.*

4. From *defending* to *embracing.*

5. From *how bad it is* to *how good we can make it.*

6. From *being right* to *being warm.*

7. From *it being about you* to *it being about them.*

Bob's next scheduled TV appearance was with Tim Russert on NBC's *Meet the Press.* A few hours before he went on the air, we spoke on the phone. I advised him that rather than concentrate on Tim, he should be thinking about the television audience *acting as if he were already president.* I told him the Dorothy Sarnoff mantra, which she—the great actress and speech coach— taught me to keep in mind before every major speech and public appearance.

"I'm glad I'm here. I'm glad you're here. I care about you. I'm in control."

Before I gave any big speeches at Avon, I used to make a point of consulting with Dorothy, who, in a long career on the stage and in films, has performed as a singer and an actor, most notably in *The King and I*. She knew what it was like to be up there. "I want you to change just one thing," I can distinctly recall her saying when I rehearsed for her a major speech I was about to give for an event at the Waldorf. "I want every single person in that audience to feel themselves in your *embrace*. I want you to include all of us, and make us all feel that you care about all of us."

When coaching Bob Graham, I said to him, "You know, the best stuff always comes from the inside out. There are a lot of people out there who can tell you how to use your hands, not so many people who can tell you how to reveal your heart. It's got to be, as in every great performance, that you are giving your audience the best gift you have."

His appearance on *Meet the Press* with Senator Richard Shelby of Alabama and California Congresswoman Nancy Pelosi was a major leap forward. He listened hard. You could see him listening. You could feel him listening. You could practically hear him listening. I helped him to look straight in his questioner's eyes. I was pleased to see him leaning *in* to the question, instead of leaning back like so many people do on these interview shows, which makes them look like hawks about to plunge on their next meal. He wasn't hunching over, which is a very different thing from leaning in. His performance, because of course that was what it was, represented a substantial step forward. On the other hand, he was still, lawyer-like, burying his lead in the conclusion. We still had our work cut out for us.

At one point, Tim Russert asked him, "What about that little notebook, Senator? What's it all about?"

"It helps me to focus; it helps me to remember," he said, but it made for a bit of an awkward moment, instead of an opportunity to score a point.

When we spoke afterward, I advised, "Next time they bring that up, talk about it as a *discipline*. You're the guy who always remembers everything that they said. Make it a tongue-in-cheek sort of thing."

We talked about the fact that, thankfully, Tim Russert had not asked him to sing the "Bob Graham for President" song written by a longtime friend and supporter and being lightly parodied in the press. We had actually considered that possibility, and I had suggested that he say, "I'd love to, Tim, if you'll sing it along with me."

"Gail, I really leaned in to it," he said proudly.

"And you had us in the palm of your hand," I replied.

We talked about the fact that the really big question was: "How can I reveal myself to these very smart, very caring, very committed people so that they can trust me and recognize me for who I am?"

Senator Graham, like a lot of successful, competent, and accomplished people, was with good reason extremely reluctant to let go of things that had worked for him in the past. I was fortunate to have Tom Gibson in my corner, who whenever Bob turned resistant would say, very simply, "Bob, walk with Gail on this. She's moving in the right direction."

A major transformation for Bob was to move from senatorial to presidential modes of expression. The Senate has been his home for sixteen years, and it is by design the deliberative body of the nation. It is not a raucous body, and by tradition, not a place where emotion rules; rationality and calm, focused decision-making are most highly valued. The Senate is not about change; it is about being resistant to change. It is the opposite of a change machine. The House is the body more deliberately re-active to the mood of the times. Members of the House are in a cycle of perpetual re-election. A senator is not supposed to be all that sensitive to change. But a presidential candidate? Now, that's a very different kettle of fish, as Senator Graham was learning on the run.

Watching Bob in action, I realized that running in a political campaign is an extremely *physical* process, not unlike training for the Olympics. It involves enormous physical effort as well as mental discipline. It involves working out, doing the laps, summoning up the energy and the dynamism to keep going, fully engaged and kinetic long after any rational person would have thrown in the towel. We talked about the idea that an extremely challenging athletic event, or even emotional event, does not always have to be draining or exhausting but something you can take energy *from*. As in any kind of transformation, you want to make sure it's a dynamic thing and that the energy comes from the change, as well as the change being a product of the energy.

We talked about the fact that people engage in typecasting—we all do—and that such classifications can be limiting. Bob, for example, used to say to audiences, "You know, I'm not the charismatic type." But did that mean that he could not be in the future? The typical view of what type you are is like a big circle, I told him. Inside that circle is absolutely everything you could develop about yourself. Every thought, thought through. Every talent developed. If you are made of colors, it contains every color in the rainbow. That is the totality of the possibilities of you.

As Bob prepared for an important debate among the Democratic candidates, to be held at New York's Pace University, I developed a habit of walking around the block with him prior to an event. It became our little ritual. I had to squeeze into a very few minutes the essence of my message to him.

Bob Graham had been an excellent senator. Did that mean he had what it takes to be a great president? I told him that this alone did not qualify him to be president—but the totality of his experiences, his passion, and his vision *did*. The challenge here was to reveal to his audience how much he cares, as opposed to how much he knows. The challenge was to show how passionate he could be, to become more open and revealing.

This was not about being uncertain, I said. It was about being certain. Debates are not about imparting information, I said; they're about conveying impressions. During the debate prep, where he worked closely with all of his aides and handlers and writers, I had just one last point to make.

"As a speaker," I said, "you can't ask an audience to *reach* for a thought. You've got to *hand* them the thought. You've got to develop the thought for them. The Dukakis problem, I said, was too many words. You've got a problem with too many words.

"You've got all the information at your fingertips," I added. "This is not about the information. This is about leading with a passionate point. This is about telling them something you care deeply about. There is no way to overdo this. There is no way to come across as too passionate or too *committed*. Don't second-guess yourself. Don't think to yourself, 'Let's not get carried away here.' *Get* carried away here."

I had two words to leave him with. "Think crisp."

At first, he looked baffled.

"Have you ever had a really great dry martini?"

Then he got it. I could see it in his eyes.

It was at that point, really quite late in the game, that we stepped back to step one in our coaching process: *Building the Castle First*. I sensed that we were getting to the root of the problem of Bob's presidential campaign, which was that he—and his campaign staff—had not really completed their homework in Building the Castle First. I understood why they hadn't, because it isn't easy, but it is a crucial step in swinging to your next trapeze, whether you are a presidential candidate or a waiter or an executive or a mom or a dad.

The big question to ask yourself in building the castle first, whatever your goal, is really quite simple:

How good can we make it?

Another way of saying the same thing is:

What would good look like?

What is driving you? What is compelling you to do this? We all need to ask ourselves this question every day of the week, and if possible, every minute of the day. With an actor, as in Method Acting, the question is always: "What is my motivation?" Obviously, Bob Graham differed from a number of players on my team in that he had already stepped into the arena, on countless occasions, and had a whole lot of ground he'd already walked on, to an extraordinary degree.

And yet, at the same time, here he was facing a new void, a new quantum leap, and I felt an empty space in his message when it came to answering that critical question: How good can we make it?

Before the debate at Pace University, I asked Tom Gibson and his wife, Suzanne, one of the candidate's four daughters, what was driving Bob to become president, what was igniting his passion. Without missing a beat, Suzanne answered that she thought her father was compelled by a commitment to fundamentally change the course of the country from what he felt was the wrong direction of the current administration in virtually every arena, from citizens' rights to homeland security to economic security. His commitment to his country was undeniable, she said. His patriotism unquestionable. His desire to help unimpeachable. What remained unexplored was the castle, which was—by the way—equally unexplored by the other candidates he was running against, all of whom were spending, from my point of view, too much time talking about the dungeons and the dragons and the crocodiles in the moat and not enough time thinking or talking or envisioning the ramparts and the flag and the beautiful hall inside with the knights and the round table. A castle is a fairy tale world of magic, to which we transport ourselves—or are transported by others. Walt Disney could do it for us. We need to be moved to be transported. And of course, it needs to be real, to be doable.

What Bob was, and we all could feel it, was *outraged*. We felt his outrage. It was genuine. But do we elect leaders because they are outraged or because they can articulate a vision for the future? This is what George Bush Sr. famously referred to as "the vision thing," and, as reflected in the awkwardness of the phrase, he badly stumbled on that one. Now, it was clear to Bob Graham, who had a highly developed sense of morality and honor, that the country felt on the wrong track. And I didn't consider it my job, by the way, to ask why he felt that way, or even to question whether it was true. As his coach, my job was to try to channel that anger and frustration into something more productive and useful than negative emotion.

What Bob was doing at that phase of the campaign was a very common phenomenon. He was being right about their being wrong. As I tell everyone I work with at various times, being right about being wrong can be an insurmountable impediment to moving forward. You can even have that carved on your tombstone after you're gone. "I was Right. They were Wrong." Yes, the world is corrupt and people are weak. But you can spend your marriage, your time as a parent, your entire life being right about how wrong it is. And you know what? Your life can go sailing right by when you're right about their being wrong. It's the most seductive role you can play. It's so absolutely delicious. Because if you take it to its logical extreme—and why not, because it is so delicious—you get to be a *martyr*. And that is *really* delicious!

Anger is human. It can also be toxic.

So I asked Bob, a little bit late in the game I have to admit, what he cared about most.

He thought about that for a bit, and said, "Beyond the essential duty of the president to ensure our national security, I care about people and jobs. I care about creating good jobs." He told me about his Workdays and how much he had learned from them. "What we really need in this country," he said, "is good jobs with good benefits." And because he was taking the step of owning the ground he had already walked on, he talked about the number of good jobs he had created in his state and how he honestly regarded that as at or near the top of his list of achievements.

"Okay," I said quickly, because we hadn't much time, "let's run with that."

Jeff Garin, Bob's pollster, liked that as a theme. "Okay," he said, "you are the 'jobs candidate.'"

So that's how Bob Graham became the jobs candidate.

With an hour to go before the debate, we were all running around with our little scraps of paper, on which we had distilled our own little messages for the candidate. Because the Senator remembers everything and has a virtually photographic memory, I knew he'd etch everything I said into his brain. Here is what I had written on my piece of paper:

"Debates are about impressions, not information."

—Aaron Brown, CNN

My favorite part about that was that as far as I knew, Aaron Brown hadn't said this at all. For my purposes, it didn't matter. He certainly *could* have said it, and remember, one of my major mantras is, *I get to decide.* That is where we get to make things up, when it suits us. It may not have been factually correct, but it was true to the spirit of what I needed to say. "Let go of the cerebral," was my basic point. "We already know you're smart. Show us your passion." And another thing he got to decide, I told him: "You're not running for president. You are *already* the president. Let them *feel* that you are the president."

I told him to dig around inside that self of his and find the spirit of his true convictions. If what you care about is creating good jobs, talk about jobs, and no matter what words you're saying, we'll *hear you*, because we'll hear the conviction in your voice. With minutes to go before he took the stage for the first round of questions, I left him with one final thought: "Talk about how good we could make it. This is America. How good can we make America, not how bad it is right now."

He told me a story I'd never heard, about his Workdays, which were obviously among the most powerful experiences of his life. He told me how, as governor, he had worked as an orderly in a nursing home alongside an elderly African-American gentleman by the name of Johnny Denton. At the end of the day, which he had spent changing soiled sheets and taking the folks to the bathroom, he said to Johnny, "You know, it's one thing for me to be doing this today, but it's another for you to be doing it every day."

Johnny Denton replied, "Governor, each day as I walk through that front door, I think to myself that God must really love these people to let them live so long. And I figure that if God loves these people, I can love them too."

I could hear in his voice that he cared deeply, passionately, about that moment. And that for Bob Graham, that moment crystallized everything he hoped about and cared about this country. I urged him to tell that story if he got the opportunity that night.

Each of the candidates had been given a classroom to convene in, but in the final few minutes, all of the candidates and all of their staffs were ushered together into the green room to have their makeup done. All of the candidates were perfectly cordial. Handsome John Edwards, who is fifty but looks thirty, was the only one of the candidates very carefully spraying his own hair. Carol Mosely Braun, the only woman in the group, at one point cracked us all up by singing, "I am woman, hear me roar."

A few minutes later, I saw that she was standing alone in a corner, looking nervous. Since she was the only woman of the group, I walked up to her and said, "You know, once you get in the water, you find you know how to swim." She smiled that smile of hers and nodded appreciatively.

Just then, Bob's extraordinary wife, Adele, turned to me just as he was about to step into the light of the cameras and said in her deep, sweet southern accent, "Gail, can't you fix his hair? There's this part sticking up."

I was just about to say that I wasn't sure that that was the most appropriate thing for me to do when some fellow came running up to him clutching a laptop computer equipped with a wireless connection.

"Senator," he said, as if delivering a message to a general in battle, "I don't want you to be blindsided by this."

Before I could stop him, the guy, out of breath, handed Bob his computer. On the screen was a late-breaking Associated Press story about how Bob wasn't doing enough to galvanize the voters. About how his campaign was running low on money, low on steam, about how many supposedly politically savvy people— the "smart money," as they always say—were already beginning to count him out.

Since I hadn't succeeded in physically separating this bearer of bad tidings from the senator, I was obliged to spring into urgent damage control mode. About ten minutes before the debate we had spent the whole day prepping him for, I could tell in his face that all of the wind had just fallen out of his sails and that it was going to be a big job to get him back into a fighting mood.

"There are some things," I said to him, very intently, looking him straight in the eye, "that are just not worth listening to. There are some things that should just get lost. There are some things that you should *edit out*." Glaring at this guy, I said to

Bob, "It really has nothing to do with tonight. It has nothing to do with this moment. This moment we're going to take to its limit."

And then, in truly my favorite moment of the night, as we walked down the back stairs of Pace University into the "holding room for the candidates," he and I spontaneously broke into a song and dance routine. Together we sang, "Give 'em the old razzle-dazzle" from *Chicago*. We did a little tap dance. Amazingly, out of the blue, it worked. It snapped him right back into his fighting spirit; the spirit of Seabiscuit was back in the room, and that awful AP article had been forgotten.

It was only a few weeks after that triumphant few hours—Bob was fabulous in the debate, the best I'd ever seen him—when I got a call from the senator. He told me that he had decided to withdraw from the race. Of course, for all of us, that decision was deeply disappointing. But we spoke for about twenty minutes, reviewing what his message would be for his announcement on *Larry King*. I knew that Roy Horn of Siegfried & Roy had just been mauled by a tiger, so that he would inevitably be sandwiched in between that and some other piece of tabloid fodder. But I said, "Never mind what Larry asks you. Talk about what you want to talk about. That you're stepping out of the race but not out of the arena. That you sincerely believe this country is suffering from a crisis of leadership, but that sometimes it takes a crisis to show us what we are, and how truly great we are, as a people."

I couldn't help feeling, as I watched the senator—no longer the candidate—on *Larry King* that night, that possibly if we had started a little earlier in the game, we could have worked together so he could come across as more dynamic and charismatic, as I knew he had the potential to be. Here was a man whom I admired tremendously for his courage, his intelligence, his credentials, his clear-headedness, his passion. The one element that had been missing in his campaign was his ability to electrify people and to connect with them emotionally. He has so many excellent qualities. He has a statesmanlike quality, an intellectual elegance. He truly has a beautiful mind. And of course, creating that sense of emotional connection can take time. He has a certain innate reserve that can be very becoming. In the midst of all the fist pounding and haranguing that accompanies a typical political season, there is a sweet spot. But if they can't hear you, that is not their fault. You can't blame the audience for not getting the message.

In the end, it was like Michelangelo sculpting his *David*. We had worked hard at taking away all the stuff that wasn't *David*. All the stuff that would have stood in his way as revealing himself to us. He had to reveal that part of himself to himself.

A day or two later, I received a handwritten letter from Bob bearing the Senatorial seal.

Gail, the star in this campaign, from my point of view, is my getting to know and to work with you. I only wish we'd met five or ten years ago. You have a great gift. You are able to reveal qualities in individuals they didn't know they had. Qualities that were always there. I can't tell you how grateful I am for that and what an incredible difference it's made in my life.

Now, that is a true star. He had stepped into the arena with grace and courage and left it with grace and courage.

Did he win or did he lose?

You tell me.

Exercise One: The Dorothy Sarnoff Method

Everyone is called upon to be a leader sometimes, as a parent, as a spouse, as a citizen, as a friend. In the end, we all have to be better leaders of our own lives. Many people have acquired the false impression that power is about imposing your will on others. But in reality, a truly powerful person is one who empowers others. In any situation where you have something at stake, repeat the Dorothy Sarnoff mantra: "I'm glad I'm here. I'm glad you're here. I care about you. I'm in control."

Exercise Two: The Bob Graham Leadership Principle

Listen to learn something new, not to be right about what you already know. Treat every event as a fact-finding mission.

Explorers, archeologists, documentary film makers, journalists, and good politicians gather facts. They don't worry about what their subject matter thinks of them—they are only concerned with what it can teach them.

Exercise Three: Candid Camera

Pretend you're making a documentary of the town you live in. We like movies because they provide an escape from ourselves. For two hours, we are completely swept into a new world, and we pay attention to every detail—every facial expression, every gesture, every raindrop. We don't think about what we're going to have for dinner, or replay the fight we had with our mother— we're too busy paying attention. So practice bringing that sense of mindfulness as you walk through your town. You can even put your favorite movie soundtrack on your Walkman to put you more in the mood. Now walk through your town and try to notice as many things as you can. Try to imagine what people on the bus are thinking about. Notice how much the flower that's popping through the crack in the sidewalk has grown. Train yourself to pay attention to your life so when that great person or opportunity comes, you'll be alert enough to see it. After your walks, record your impressions in your journal.

THE JAZZ
GUITARIST

"MANY GUITARISTS LEAP FROM LEAN plucks to shattering swing fluently, but not all of them create breezy atmospheres that rouse the romantic and chill the cynic. . . . Mazza's amazing, with an absorbingly original taste for decorating classical chords with a choppy, colorful, bracing jazz vocabulary that's deeply hypnotic." —*The Village Voice*

"You've got to know your stuff to play in one of the city's premier intimate guitar rooms, and local jazz guitarist Peter Mazza certainly fits. His lyrical side really comes to the fore when he takes off on a solo flight. And the best thing is that his knowledge of jazz and pop standards is encyclopedic." —*Time Out New York*

If I were a club owner, I'd want to hire him. Within several minutes of meeting Peter Mazza, he told me that he was thirty-four, and that for all his acclaim—"recognized for his passionate and poignant interpretations of the most complex jazz standards," as it said on his Web site—he was still basically living from gig to gig. It felt like his life was a constant struggle to achieve an artistic and commercial breakthrough. He needed to figure out some better way to structure his artistic life, he added, or else he needed to find something else to do with it, quickly.

I had learned from a brief perusal of his Web site before he came in that by "blending clean and fluent lines with colorful and inventive chord voicings, he creates lush solo guitar pieces as well as imaginative ensemble arrangements." I learned that he was born and raised in New York City, that he was encouraged to pursue his interest in music by his father, an accomplished amateur jazz pianist who later became a creative director for a major advertising agency. And I learned that he has played alongside such acclaimed jazz greats as Brad Mehldau, Chris Potter, Larry Goldings, Christian McBride, Greg Hutchinson, Roy Hargrove, Kurt Rosenwinkel, Paul Bollenback, Jack Wilkins, Freddie Bryant, and Jonathan Kreisberg.

I include that long list of names, by the way, to make a point. These are some of the best-known and respected jazz musicians in New York City and, with the possible exception of Roy Hargrove, I hadn't heard of a single one of them. (Have you?) And I happen to love jazz. Peter's road to artistic success was not going to be an easy one, given that he can rise to the very top of his field and still remain comparatively obscure to the general public. If you're in country music, it's easy to want to be the next Johnny Cash or Loretta Lynn; if you're in rock, the next Bono or Sting. But if you're a jazz musician, your idols are likely to be Pat Metheny, John Scofield, Pat Martino, Jim Hall, and Mark Whitfield, all of whom served on a prestigious panel of judges for the Thelonious Monk Jazz Competition in which Peter placed as a semifinalist in 1996. Of these, only the first ranks as anything close to a household name.

When I finally did meet Peter in person, one of the first things that struck me about him was his extremely articulate presentation, a trait that stood out in my mind because so many musicians I have met over the years tend to speak with their own private idioms, which often connect them more closely to each other, but cut them off from the rest of us. The clarity and expressiveness of his music were reflected in his ability to communicate verbally. His initial presentation reminded me of the music I'd heard on his Web site: cool, crisp, clean, and precise, with a strong tinge of the cerebral and analytical. These are, of course, generally positive characteristics, whether your goal is to be a successful rocket scientist, brain surgeon, financier, politician, or musician. But when it comes to coaching and changing and jumping to the next level, swinging out onto your next trapeze, sometimes these traits can become significant impediments. As I've said before—and will say again—the fun and the juice and the kick are not in the knowing, but in the *not knowing*. An extremely intelligent person can be highly skilled at rationalizing just about anything under the sun, including the need not to change. An extremely intelligent person can sometimes defend their home turf with the tenacity of a seasoned trial lawyer.

I would have to describe Peter as a little ill at ease at first, and above all, extremely certain and exact about what his life should be like, what his choices were and what they were not, and quite precise about what role music should play in that life. If nothing else, I felt compelled to shake things up a little bit. All those things he took for granted, as givens? He didn't know it yet, but after a few sessions with me, he was going to be throwing all that stuff out the window. He thought he knew what he knew? Hah! Before he could say lickety-split, he would be realizing that he didn't know anything, really, for sure. And that would be a great starting point for his big jump—our platform to leap for the stars.

I jotted down a single word on my notepad: *Rigid*. Then I crossed out that word and wrote: *Stringent*. Then I kept listening, saying at first very little. Peter told me, pretty much right off the bat, that he couldn't help it, but he felt a need to become the sort of adult who could maintain a middle-class lifestyle, and possibly at one point, a family. He was not immediately interested in starting a family, but he was immediately interested in getting a life that didn't preclude having one at some point. One of the rigid notions that he was clinging to (for dear life) was that life was presenting him with an either/or proposition. He either had to make it—big—as an artist, or else be consigned to a life of failure. That was one of the dichotomies in his mind that immediately struck me as worth taking a closer look at.

STEP ONE: BUILD THE CASTLE FIRST

We started by building the castle first. For this exercise, I've found that a schematic diagram approach is useful. I draw a circle—a big circle—and I say to whomever it is I'm talking with that inside that circle is absolutely everything you could develop about yourself. Every thought, thought through. Every talent developed. Every color, if it contained colors, filled in. That circle represents, I say, *the totality of the possibilities of you.*

"How much do you think you've explored about yourself?" I always ask.

The typical answer: "Oh, about 80 percent."

I wish I had a little buzzer, like they do on the game shows. *Buzz! Wrong!*

In fact, I insist, it's really more like 15 percent, because those great white spaces on the map are unexplored territory, terra incognita, the landscapes and valleys not only not yet explored, but ones you don't even realize exist. That is the magical realm, the void that lies between your trapezes, the particular ones that your particular life has chosen to dangle in your path. "We don't know what we don't know," I say, and I mean it. "How much do we *really* know about the fullness of the possibilities of our life?" Who we really are is often not the same thing as who we think we are.

Think of all the pet phrases—the clichés—that people say, without really thinking, that sum up and subtly reinforce the conventional wisdom that change, when it comes, is something dangerous and messy and, above all, to be avoided like the plague. *Stick to your knitting.* Now what on earth does that mean? I personally think that is one of the least useful sentiments anyone can ever articulate, yet people say it as if they've just discovered something very wise. I suppose that it means, in business-school jargon, "Let's stick to our core competency." Boy, I've heard that one a lot in my time. *We make our own beds and lie in them.* What in the world does *that* mean? Does it mean, for example, that we can't ever change the sheets? I actually do believe, by the way, that we shouldn't *cry over spilled milk*, because it is a real waste of our precious time to endlessly wallow in the failures of the past. But if somebody tells me with a straight face, *If it ain't broke, don't fix it*, it makes me want to ring their neck. Why not fix it if it ain't broke? Is there a law against making things better, or a law stating that all things must stay the same? How about, *That's not the way we do it around here?* Or the

British upper-crust version, *That, my dear, is just not the done thing?*

When I asked Peter to describe his castle in detail, his answer was short and sweet. To the question of "What would good look like?" he thought for a moment. "I would never be worried," he said, with an anxious sigh, "about getting the next gig." For those blessed—or cursed—with the freedom of freelancing, there is always a very fine line between freedom and fear. It becomes so easy, in this vulnerable spot, to let your mind play tricks on you. When work slows down, the doubting voices inside your head will often triumphantly proclaim, "See? You will never get another piece of work in your life." And Peter's problems in this area were only amplified by the fact that it is possible to be a successful thriving musician—as he was—working all the time, and still feel as if you are fighting an uphill battle for creative expression and artistic success.

One solution to this problem, in my experience, is to widen one's creative and artistic horizons so that—like a stock portfolio—your capabilities more naturally diversify. So many people of an artistic and creative persuasion tend to construct what they believe to be their authentic selves and lock it away in an airtight box, which they defend like a fortress under constant siege. "Don't go in that box," their body language announces when you raise the subject, "Don't even go *near* that box. Most important of all, *Don't try to open that box.* That, you see, is Pandora's Box. Open it, and that closely guarded real self will die.

But life is full of curious paradoxes, one of which is that creative people who don't tend to regard themselves as being "in business" are, in fact, in business, whether they like it or not. Can you imagine, if you've never done it yourself (God knows I have), having to get up in the morning and literally every day of your life be out there hustling and humping and pounding the pavements, all to get someone to pay you for what you love to do best? Of course, one answer to that problem is perfectly obvious: Get a job. But getting a job often requires that you relinquish your dream, and Peter was nowhere near that stage yet.

That night, Peter made a list of ten things that would constitute his dream life. I encouraged him not to hold back, but to include elements from his personal as well as professional life, as a means of achieving a healthier work/life balance.

"If anything were possible," he wrote, "I would:

1. Have millions in the bank.

2. Be in great health and have a great diet/exercise/training program.

3. Compete in a martial arts tournament.

4. Own my own successful company.

5. Write a book.

6. Have a hit CD of original music.

7. Win a presidential award for my playing and writing or work with people.

8. Create and establish my own concept of musical therapy.

9. Run a fitness/wellness center that teaches principles of positive thinking and fitness therapy.

10. Own a beautiful loft in NYC and a beautiful home in the country.

During our next session, we talked a little more about what *building the castle first* would mean for Peter. He was hoping one day that a big jazz record label would come to him and recognize him for who he was. "You're Peter Mazza!" they'd say. "We want to distribute your CD. We want to put you on tour. We want to make you a star." He was also hoping to seek out promotional deals from instrument companies, which provide musicians with high-end guitars, for example, in exchange for the musicians' endorsement. We talked about the fact that what would be good—not just good, but *great*—would be for him to be able to compose his own original music and to create his own signature sound—to become, in effect, his own brand. That's what would get him those recording and endorsement deals that he so yearned for. That's what would get him out of the low-paying rut of just playing from gig to gig and make him what he truly wanted to be, what every performer wants to be: a star. And we talked about the possibility of being more commercial—

without diminishing himself—in other ways, to take enough of the pressure off himself *to let himself be free*, a virtual prerequisite to being a star.

STEP TWO: OWN THE GROUND
YOU'VE ALREADY TRAVELED

During our first consultation, Peter had mentioned, in passing, as if it were something to be ashamed of, that he had been ranked as a semi-finalist in the prestigious Thelonious Monk Jazz Competition by a panel comprised of some of the best jazz musicians in the world. As someone who narrowly missed qualifying for the Olympics by three-quarters of a second, I know what that feels like—to just miss the big time. Still, I was surprised to hear that Peter wasn't able to appreciate the level of success that finishing as a semi-finalist in the most prestigious jazz competition in the country indicated. Let's just say that it sounded pretty darn good to me. Even great. But to Peter—or rather that old Peter who first stepped through my door, a Peter who arguably no longer exists, although occasionally he revives from time to time, to nettle and pester the new Peter—the incontrovertible *fact* that really mattered was the one that told him that he had *not won*. Can't argue with that, right? Wrong. In fact, you can. Because you can argue that what Peter made of that was a false and self-defeating interpretation. When he first walked through my door, he was convinced that being a semi-finalist in this particular contest meant that he was doomed to fail.

Sounds crazy, right? But you may not have yet met up with a true perfectionist, for whom anything less than perfection is a mortal sin. In an attempt to straighten this one out before we moved on, I walked him through the distinction of *fact* versus *interpretation*. Talk about owning the ground you've already traveled on—this was a perfect case in point. I told Peter that I could personally guarantee that for at least one of the finalists in the Thelonious Monk competition, the important fact was that he or she hadn't won the competition. And that even for the person who actually won, I could feel fairly confident that that person was thinking to themselves, when they handed him or her the trophy, "Whew! I really slipped that one by, didn't I? What about the next time? *What if the next time is the time that I really screw up?*"

See what I mean? By constantly imbuing these facts with meaning and letting meaning and interpretation indiscriminately blend together, we douse our own flames and do ourselves all sorts of grave disservices. I told Peter that what mattered most in such cases was to take the peak of your career success and lead from that. Because too many of us lead from the troughs. *When you're pitching a project and they don't call you back, well, you know why, don't you?* It's because you weren't good enough, right? Maybe yes, maybe no. But the important thing is, what's the point of making it mean anything more than it has to mean? When they don't call back, it could very well be that the entire project was cancelled, or that they were forced to hire the brother-in-law of a board member. But we are constantly letting those sniping critics that sit on our shoulders hold sway over our personal universes.

As Albert Einstein once said, "If the facts don't fit the theory, change the facts." The Romantic poets used to say very much the same thing when they talked about "fact versus fancy," which is just an old-fashioned term for making things up. Being something of a latter-day Romantic poet myself, the way that I prefer to put it is that yes, there are facts, but we *get to decide* what those facts *mean*. The poet John Keats, in a letter to his brother in 1817, coined the phrase "negative capability," which he insisted was a prerequisite for any great poet or artist. Keats defined this ideal state of mind as when a person "is capable of being in uncertainties, mysteries, doubts, without any irritable reaching after fact and reason."

Now, there's a sentiment I can wholeheartedly endorse. Because it is precisely that "irritable reaching after fact and reason" that ultimately lets so many of us insist that it is a "fact" that you never make it as a ____(fill in the blank). Or, "I'll never get married because I'm over thirty-five and less than 10 percent of women over thirty-five ever get married." Or, "I'll never get that perfect job where I say to myself, 'I can't believe that they're paying me to do this.'" What Keats meant by "negative capability" is, in fact, maintaining an imaginative openness to the infinite possibilities of life when faced with uncertainty, "without any irritable reaching after fact and reason."

Another Romantic poet, Samuel Taylor Coleridge, meant much the same thing when he coined the phrase "willing suspension of disbelief." In the introduction to his first book of poems, Coleridge observed that while his dear friend William Wordsworth was publishing realistic poems about ordinary people, he himself seemed compelled to write about more fantastic things, steeped in the well of his imagination, from "Kubla Khan" to "The Rime of the Ancient Mariner" to "Christabel," none of which were in the slightest bit ordinary or about ordinary people. He begged his readers to permit him "that willing suspension of disbelief for the moment that constitutes poetic faith." Ever since, we have used that wonderful expression to describe what all of us do when watching a play or a movie or reading a book. We *suspend our disbelief* that we are *in fact* inhabiting an imaginary world. But what if we apply that same sensibility to our own supposedly "real" world and suspend our disbelief that these supposed "facts" of our life are so darned determinative?

I suggested that Peter could use the concepts presented by the Romantic poets in expanding his own artistic possibilities. "In assembling the person that is the new Peter," I reminded him at one point, "I don't think anybody out there has the *faintest idea* of the final definition of what good is, as it pertains to you personally. If you present your new self with all of your heart and all of your soul and faith that you are that person, that will carry you through." That is the willing suspension of disbelief. That is negative capability. Or, to put it a bit more colloquially: Fake it till you make it.

STEP THREE: LET GO

One of the first things that I felt Peter would be better off letting go of was his Romantic quest for security. I call it a Romantic quest because I sincerely believe that today, security is a figment of our imagination, of nostalgia and wishful thinking. Today, I told him, very few of us really possess any degree of job security, personal security, financial security, or national security. The idea of a career path is, to many of us, a bad joke. Not that many of us don't have good jobs and don't keep them and don't like them, but the idea that this is a given has been thrown right out the window. So what do we have left? Our own capacity for self-reinvention, which permits us—compels us—to plow ahead, despite, or even because of, the uncertainties that lie ahead.

Peter made a list of his personal "letting goes," starting out with the idea of having to be perfect, of knowing it all. Trust that you are *already* good, and let go that those hanging judges on your shoulders that are always telling you the truth when they say, "You'll never make it, why don't you quit while you're behind?" So many of us are waiting to be discovered and recognized for who *we really are*. In Peter's case, he was waiting to be discovered by the powers-that-be in the music industry and recognized as a superb jazz guitarist. But surprise, surprise: he had already been recognized as such—both by the critics as well as by his peers. But he hadn't explicitly recognized *himself* as such. The problem with perfectionism is that it makes nothing good enough. Of course, one could argue that that's what compels perfectionists to always get better, but in fact, it more often puts us in a deep funk, because in our distorted minds, we can never be good enough, so why bother?

In some ways, it takes a certain blissful naïveté to not acknowledge the demons and the dangers when you climb to the top of that pedestal and look down into the void. When I first moved to New York, I had no idea how hard it was supposed to be to get a job or how long it was supposed to take to find an apartment. If I had done a flow chart or a pie chart or run statistics on how many other young women were moving to New York that very same year, or even that very same month, or looking for work at the same time, or looking for an apartment, I would have been tempted to throw in the towel right from the beginning. Fortunately, life is not like that. Once you start believing in statistics, it's almost impossible to believe in yourself. It's more difficult to be motivated, inspired, optimistic, energized about the future, because we accept these supposed facts as the truth, the whole truth, and nothing but the truth, so help us God.

When I saw him next, Peter proudly presented me with his personal throw-away list.

1. I *have* to be a musician.

2. I *have* to be an unconditional virtuoso.

3. I am not a great musician.

4. I am not successful.

5. I am incapable of understanding the technology.

6. I am not capable of understanding financial things.

7. I am not capable of learning new things.

8. My mental hard drive is limited.

9. Beauty and depth lie in technique and appearances.

10. I have to practice constantly.

11. I am not deep or beautiful.

12. Other people know more than me.

13. Money and success are bad and selfish.

14. I can't be successful financially.

15. I can't have creative/financial/political views and goals.

16. I can't look foolish or unknowledgeable.

17. I'll look stupid and unknowledgeable if I try new things—dancing, cooking, singing.

18. I have to like everyone.

19. Everyone has to like me.

20. I always have to be right.

21. I am, in fact, always wrong.

One of the most important old assumptions we added to Peter's throw-away list was: "Playing music is mainly a matter of absorbing a lot of data and personalizing and processing it." Peter, by his own admission, tended to spend too much time on the instrument itself, "which was a safe space for me to be in," he later recalled.

I loved hiding in the purely technical and mechanical side of the equation, which I intuitively understood was endangering my ability to grow as an artist. In some sense, when I first came to Gail it felt like I was emotionally and psychologically at the end of my rope—my trapeze. I was fully prepared to leave music. Primarily, I needed to make money, but I was also hoping to clarify myself creatively. What Gail urged me to do was to clear away some free space inside myself before I came to any grand conclusions about the direction of the future. I had to try to create some space for the new me.

Once again, not unlike Bob Graham, Peter had to let go of everything he knew and feel the passions that drove him. He had to let go of the wealth of knowledge he'd gained analytically and intellectually, in order to flow with his soul and his guts and his blood. With Bob Graham, I had pointed out that if his speech patterns were music, the composer would have written *legato* in the margins. What he really needed to do was take a deep breath and let it *flow* out of him. I gave the same advice to Peter that I did to Bob Graham and, in fact, anyone trying to get a message across to the public, in whatever medium. To Peter, I tried to put it in his language—that he had to let the jazz part of jazz take over and the intellectual mind disappear.

Peter was very involved with the idea of music as data and information. He had formulated an almost cybernetic conception of his art. I wrote a little note to myself. "Less needing to know. More open to serendipity. Less analytical, more experiential." And during that same session, Peter wrote a little note to himself: "I've learned a language from a textbook. Now I need to learn not only how to speak it in simple declarative sentences, but how to write poetry in it."

"Letting go," I told Peter at one point, "is really more of an editing process, which means that there are a lot of things that are good to keep." One of those things, I believed, was his sense of himself as mainly a musician, as wholly a musician, because that, in the rock bottom place, was where his true passion lay and where he was, where he lived. What he had to do moving forward was to redefine his role as a musician, to open it up to other possibilities and prospects.

At the time, I jotted down a little note to myself:

Moving Peter from the finely analytical weighing of pros and cons. The whole technical aspect of what he does has to fade away so you can hear the passion shine through. Very parallel, oddly enough, to Bob Graham. One again, the focus needs to be on intuition and cutting the analyzing. Whether you're speaking or playing an instrument, it's important not to judge yourself at the time and in the moment. The best way is not to weigh the value of what you're saying while you say it.

Meanwhile, after the same session, Peter wrote in *his* notes:

Avoid casting blame on others. Accept responsibility for not finishing book or CD, for not pursuing other interesting career possibilities, for failing to see that the world is full of options. I've wanted to crash and burn. I'm dramatic and shy and proud. It's not dad's fault. It's not mom's fault. It's not the jazz world's fault. To want is very dangerous and very daunting. Wants: great job, interests, hobbies, new pace, great relationship.

Another image that I find useful in locating these other directions is the maypole, with strands flying out in many directions, yet all attached at the top to the core, which is your guiding vision. In contemplating these other possibilities that might make up the redefinition of his artistic life, we focused on one overwhelming theme: listening.

"I'm not talking about selling out," I told him, to allay his anxieties about where this was going, and where I was coming from. "I'm talking about *moving* out." By listening, I was talking about widening those circles, widening his horizons, to encompass other possibilities of things to do with his music with which he might have fun and possibly make some money. We wrote down a few strands in Peter's life:

1. Performing classical jazz in clubs and performing at other types of events.

2. Performing original music (signature sound) at festivals and in any venue where the music is the focal point.

3. Teaching the language of music at musical colleges.

4. Teaching workshops for individual executives and management using music and jazz and improvisation as the metaphor for the creative process.

I told him that the goal was trying to define himself without losing himself. For example, here was a wild and crazy idea—about as crazy as Bob Graham becoming charismatic: "I was thinking about singing a song," he said tentatively.

"A singer . . ." I mused, intrigued by the notion. But then his resistance crept up on him again. "When I hear music," he said fatalistically, "I always listen for the notes," as if this fact somehow foreclosed the possibility of his ever becoming a singer. We discussed the possibility that singing—a little—might permit him to connect with his audience more directly, in a quirky, less "trained" way.

"Try listening for the lyrics—they're sort of like notes," I urged him. Learning the lyrics and not just the notes was all part of *widening out without selling out.* "We're revealing to you what you really love. The way you're going to play your music. The way you're going to be heard by your audience. The way you're going to step into your power."

Like most artists on earth, Peter is perpetually concerned about selling out. But I pointed out that perhaps that was one concept he would be better off shedding, like a snake does its skin. It's too narrow and insufficiently liberating. This is not about wanting to move away from the music, but moving toward it, I said. There is always that carping, sniping voice muttering in your ear, "Well, if you were really any good at this stuff, you'd be a lot more successful. You must not be any good."

Peter felt curiosity mixed with a certain degree of doubt about this new approach. "But I'm not a singer," he protested at one point.

But then I told him about the Hollywood producer who gave Fred Astaire a screen test and wrote his report at the end: "Can't sing. Dances a little." What about Louis Armstrong, Neil Young, or Bob Dylan? I asked. Did any one of those guys, when he was young, consider himself a natural-born singer? The sort of singing I was talking about was not like a singer who regards himself as primarily as singer, but like a singer who does it offhandedly because he knows he does something else really well, like dance or play the trumpet. The example I used was Herb Alpert singing, "This Guy," which was hauntingly effective (and very popular) precisely because he obviously didn't consider himself a singer. He was a trumpet player. But when he sang, we heard in the song something very different—something honest and touching—from what we would expect from a "standard" professional vocalist.

Here was yet another case of something that we think is written in stone actually being written in sand. Peter ended up really warming to the idea of expressing himself in a way that communicated vulnerability—being deliberately "unschooled" and more intuitive than analytical, combined with his compelling degree of expertise. He decided that he might try singing "Funny Valentine," not like a singer but like a guitar player who just happens to sing. He then began to debate going to a voice coach, and I encouraged him to exercise caution, because he didn't really need to sound like Bobby Darin.

While we were opening up to new ideas and letting go of old ones, we discussed the possibility of making his potential audience broader. One of the old ways of thinking to which he was particularly attached was that he wanted his music to be approved by the jazz cognoscenti, which, of course, represented, at best, a tiny percentage of his potential audience. What if we could make his target audience a bit more numerous than the small group of aficionados who hang out at the Blue Note? Would that really be such a terrible thing? After all, he had played holiday parties for the Oppenheimer Group without diminishing his artistic stature. What if he could develop an entire network for playing corporate parties for Bear Stearns or JP Morgan? He even spoke about striding confidently into the great hall at Bergdorf Goodman's and playing the guitar, all in the service of opening new markets, new opportunities for exposure, and even new opportunities for artistic growth.

One potential opportunity for expansion in this area was provided by his teaching career. Since graduating from the Manhattan School of Music in 1990, Peter has taught guitar at the

American Institute of Guitar in midtown Manhattan as the school's principal jazz instructor. Located not far from Lincoln Center and Carnegie Hall, but also not far from the office population of the city, the school is attended by a high percentage of professional people who happen to love music—and want to learn to play the guitar better, not necessarily to further a musical career, but because they take an amateur's delight in mastering a craft. With so many professional people attending his classes and taking private lessons, Peter has over the years created ample opportunities for hundreds of nonprofessionals to open themselves up to a part of themselves that would have otherwise remained unexplored due to their consuming commitment to their full-time careers. Having learned so much about the value of providing a musical accompaniment to these professionals' "other" lives, he spotted a new opportunity by more creatively tapping that market. One possibility that we discussed would be for him to branch out into delivering lectures to corporate executives, using jazz and creativity as a metaphor for innovation.

One of Peter's notes directly addressed this issue:

I have a viable career in music as a teacher—strong positive emotional presence. There is a genuine connection between my own passion, experience, ability in subject matter, and my students' desire to share and achieve same.

Good things about teaching:

It brings out people's belief in their ability to learn and experience music. I want to inspire people to tap into their intuition and not be limited by knowledge. Great artists fuse a command and sensitivity to the musical language and tools with a desire and an ability to communicate with an audience's own feelings and ideas.

STEP FOUR: FLY INTO THE VOID

I recently had a session with Peter before he played at an annual corporate function, which I was scheduled to emcee, at the Pierre Hotel. Peter was a little bit nervous, anticipating the need, as he so aptly put it, "to strike a comfortable middle ground between the carpet of sound and having an impact on the audience." At the same time, he was looking forward to playing a room filled with so many successful professional women.

At the same time, he realized that "having to play a different kind of gig can be helpful in developing these new ideas, in rising to a new level." He mentioned that he had recently made a decision to "only play what I mean and throw away the rest." He knew that he had "a tendency to present myself with a focus on technical excellence. But this event," he decided, "was really kind of a dress rehearsal for the new, potential fully blown me."

I told him that what it all boiled down to was a question of letting go of the specific expectation that there was any one way to come across, in any given situation. At the same time, and for the same event, I had decided to take a leaf out of my own book and cast myself a little bit against type and take a few risks with my presentation. For so many years, I had considered myself "the corporate type" and had dressed the part and acted it to a tee. But now I realized that, not unlike Peter, I was free to explore new aspects of my personality that I had left unexplored during that phase of my life. I was due to make a short, funny speech and introduce the main honoree, Gail King, Oprah Winfrey's best friend. I surprised myself by being nervous about it. But my husband had said, "Don't be silly. This is like falling off a log for you."

I decided to take a few chances. I decided to do something different. I saw an outfit by Donna Karan with a short ivory satin skirt, an ivory top, and beige high heels. I asked my husband what he thought of it. He took one look at me and said, "Isn't this supposed to be a breakfast?"

I was interested in projecting a different image. Sexier. Less corporate. So I bought the outfit. When I showed up, everyone I worked with was a little bit taken aback.

"Oh my God," one woman said, "you look *so* different."

What did that mean? Did that mean better? Or did that mean worse? Since I knew it was up to me to decide, I made a decision that that meant better. A lot better.

Peter was fabulous, by the way. I couldn't have been more

thrilled. I thought I was pretty good too. When I got back to my office I got an e-mail from Gail King, saying, "It was a great event and you were terrific. But what I really want to talk about is *your outfit.*"

It was a little thing, really, but I took a chance to make a little change, and I felt different. I was determined in a small way to not play it safe. I was determined to no longer be "the tailored type." I was answering the question, "How would you act if you were not the tailored type?" If you were not the shy type? If you were not whichever type you think you are and would rather not be?

Hearing Peter play for us, I could hear the signature sound. Coming out right there loud and clear. I could hear him developing the Peter Brand, with a style and an attitude and a sensibility all of its own. I could feel him, from the podium, letting go of trying to be better than Player X, some peer or role model or star. Instead, I could hear him listening—strange as that might sound—to his own distinctive signature style.

I sent him an e-mail after the event.

Date: Mon, 24 Nov 2003

Subject: Perfect

Peter!

You really were terrific. You struck exactly the right chord . . . Everyone loved your (& Johanne's) playing and I was so proud of you. I told several people that you're available for corporate events and their eyes lit up . . .

Thanks, my friend. You're wonderful.

Gail

Almost immediately, I got an e-mail back:

From: Peter Mazza

Hey Gail,

That's was GREAT!!! Thank YOU so much for having me, and for your note here. I don't always know how my music is received when it's functioning as background to these sorts of events, but it's a pleasure to hear that people were appreciative. Regardless of whether it is the focal point or not, I always offer it sincerely from my heart, with gratitude . . .

I'm really looking foreword to being in full swing with all the things we've discussed. I DO hope that some interests/things will evolve from this, so feel free to foreword all my info to whomever and/or to put me in touch with them.

Well . . . I know I have a lot of work ahead . . . I really need to listen for the ringing of my inner joyful noise or cosmic sound, so that I can ENJOY it and PLAY it. THAT ability, paired with skills I will learn from knowing you, will be my winning formula for really touching people.

That stuff is the "juice" as I think you'd say?

Anyway, be well and be in touch,

Peter

Exercise One: Be a Natural

Try to think "easy." For many people this is surprisingly not easy, because the smarter we are, the harder we make it. Think of yourself as a "natural," rather than as someone who has to work hard at being good. Make a list of things that you consider "hard" for you to accomplish. Is that fact or interpretation? Chances are it's all interpretation. Be a Romantic poet and suspend disbelief. Identify your strengths and build on them; eventually your weaknesses will be obliterated.

Exercise Two: Seek Joy over Approval

Take a look at whose "seal of approval" you are seeking. Your mother's? Your father's? Your neighbors'? Your friends'? If you get it, will that really do it for you? Then what? How much time are you wasting seeking their approval when you could be deriving joy from just doing it? If you allow yourself to play your own particular music—and I mean music in the metaphorical sense—just for the joy of it, you may reach a level of virtuosity that you never thought imaginable.

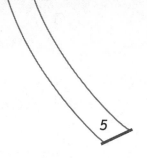

THE PHILOSOPHER
IN THE ENEMY
CAMP

"It is not the strongest of the species that survive,
nor the most intelligent, but the one most
responsive to change."
—*Charles Darwin*

I FIRST SAW ANDRES SERRANO on closed-circuit TV, helping to conduct a video-linked town meeting, in which fifty thousand employees from around the world watched him give a live presentation on the prospect of transforming a large chunk of his company's business into the digital realm. The first thing that struck me about Andres, to be perfectly frank, was that he is extremely good-looking, sort of a cross between Cary Grant and

Caesar Romero. The second thing that struck me about him was
that he seemed awfully disengaged from the proceedings. His delivery was flat, his sentences jerky, and he tended to let his points
trail off at the end without leading up to a punch. He kept
throwing away his best lines. At the same time, I felt a lot of
warmth, a lot of charm, a lot of intelligence, and really good energy. After a few minutes of watching him, I jotted down a few
notes.

"Warm. Shy? Maybe a little bit flip . . ."

I knew that a key part of my engagement with Andres would be
helping him with his presentation style. But it had also been my
experience that presentation and communication problems tend
to reflect deeper, even existential, issues. This was certainly the
case with him. I noted that he was leaning back in his chair instead
of leaning into the discussion. I wrote down some more notes:

Don't act like you just blew in for a few minutes and are just waiting
to blow back out again. You are *reporting* instead of *telling* a story. I
don't feel enough passion in your delivery. You sound too dutiful. You
need to show that you can trust other people. What I am sensing
feels more like disdain. You can't afford to just *run* the business. You
have to communicate that you *own* the business and are committed
to your team.

About two weeks before, I had received a call from the head of
the human resources department of Andres' firm, who told me

that one of the smartest, most talented men in her division, if not the entire company, had recently been brought back to their Boston headquarters from a senior post overseas and was having a difficult time adjusting to his new environment. When I asked what environment she was referring to, Amy assured me that aside from the environment at headquarters, the general environment inside her company was in a state of perpetual change. As a result, all sorts of good people were getting caught in the back draft, which made her job all the more frustrating and difficult. Andres, this highly regarded executive, had been caught in a wave of corporate turbulence not of his own making and was now being forced to pay a high price, personally and professionally, for his adjustment problems.

The long and the short of it was that the really big job Andres had been asked to take on in Boston, the really big job for which he had been induced to give up a great position managing the firm's operations throughout Europe, had been so dramatically transformed by the time he showed up at headquarters that it wasn't the same job at all. Needless to say, it hadn't changed for the better.

I couldn't help groaning. It all sounded so depressingly familiar. In my more than twenty years at Avon, I couldn't begin to count the number of times that, with all the best intentions in the world, we in senior management had promoted some swiftly rising star who had been absolutely outstanding in the field to a cushy headquarters job back in New York. Too often, once not so comfortably settled in at our home office, these extremely talented individuals ended up sinking rather than swimming. Like many animal species, humans do not always respond well to an abrupt shift of environment.

In many respects, Andres's story was not a new tale, but an old saga with a contemporary twist. Andres's highly competitive financial firm was the sort of place that has become increasingly common since the advent of reengineering and corporate makeovers. In fact, the entire organization takes a certain degree of professional pride in shooting even its most senior people in and out of slots with tremendous velocity and volatility. It's their way, they say, of shaking things up and keeping folks fresh. This is all very well and good, but if not handled correctly, artificially induced change can create havoc in individuals whose natural tolerance for flux is limited. Globalization and consolidation have placed a premium on people's capacities to survive and even thrive in a state of perpetual motion and change. The ancient Greek philosopher Heraclitus (circa 500 B.C.) seems to have pretty well nailed the twenty-first century when he said: "All is flux," "The only constant is change," and "No one steps into the same river twice." Well, certainly not at this company.

In Andres's case, the great job he had been promised by top management in the home office had never materialized. What had materialized instead was a radically rethought divisional structure in which Andres, as opposed to running his own show, was going to have to submit to a power-sharing situation with two other people all on the same level, all of whom reported to a senior executive who for many years had been Andres's best friend, mentor, and patron. Both Andres and Alberto, his mentor—the proud author of this awkward setup—were originally from Barcelona and were proud, passionate Catalonians by nature. In an attempt to avoid even the slightest hint of favoritism, Alberto had been much harder on Andres than he would otherwise have been. But while the boss was pretty tough on his former protégé, Andres's jealous colleagues simply couldn't get the idea out of their heads that he had a special relationship with their boss. As a result, they did what they could to undercut him at every conceivable opportunity.

What most irked Amy, the head of human resources for his division, was that the company had taken this rising star and failed to put him in a position where he could shine. "If we had put together a corporate property chart with all our top people ranked on it in order of potential value to the company," she said with a sigh, "Andres would have been right at the top." But now, if senior management didn't do something to intervene quickly, she worried, Andres stood a very real chance of, as she put it, "crashing and burning."

Right from the start I knew that Andres and I would have our work cut out for us. This company needed Andres to open up and not to feel in any way threatened. They needed him to feel as if he had a partner in this process. That partner, obviously, was going to be me. Before even setting up our first appointment,

I found myself thinking about what a story like his meant, in the larger sense of reflecting the controversial role that big companies are playing in society today. Despite what many of us think of them, big companies are not only here to stay but likely to get bigger, as mergers and acquisitions and industry consolidations create a corporate culture in which big companies dominate entire industries, as well as the lives of the millions of people affected by them. While the most powerful of these companies seem to relish cultivating a certain swashbuckling ruthlessness in their treatment of customers and employees alike, viewing them as tradable and replaceable commodities, I've found that some of the more enlightened large companies' apparent callousness is sometimes leavened by a pragmatic realization that human capital is an expensive investment worth protecting.

One of the best ways that companies can seek to protect and enhance that investment is to encourage executives whom they feel might benefit from it to undergo a course of executive coaching. Leading-edge companies today know that brilliant people choose *you*, you don't choose them. To acquire a reputation as a bad place to work is bad news for everyone. If people get the idea that your company is a place that encourages failure, you are likely to fail as a company. On the other hand, the deep sense of loyalty and commitment that companies once showed their employees as a matter of course has everywhere become a relic of the past. Today's companies make you a deal. *We can't be motivated to commit to you, but you'd better be motivated to*

*commit to us, or else we might eliminate not just your position,
but your entire division.*

One of the few islands of sanity and repose in these monstrous
operations can sometimes be found in the human resources de-
partments, where the people are actually getting paid to care
about other people. "There was a time that people inside this
company knew who they were and what they had to do, and
they did it without thinking a lot about it," Amy told me. "There
was a time when we thought we knew everything, and we didn't
need to learn *anything*. Now the goal is to become a community
of learners and listeners."

At the same time, she conceded, the corporate environment in
which they were all obliged to function encouraged a certain
amount of cutthroat competition, corporate infighting, and jock-
eying for power. In her organization, plenty of people take a palpable pride in besting their colleagues in these modern-day
equivalents of tournament jousts. From the CEO on down, this
sort of aggressive behavior gets rewarded, even as, contradicto-
rily, management prattles on about team play and collaboration.
A form of intense Darwinian competition is the rule.

Getting down to brass tacks, Amy observed that, in her
opinion, Andres's problems were part structural—caused by
flaws in the corporate structure—part personal, part cultural,
and part communications related. "Here's a brilliant and charismatic guy," she stressed, "who's been having trouble getting
what he needs to say out of his brain, through his mouth, and

into the ears of the people who need to hear him." One of the root causes of this problem, she admitted, was that he all too often spoke straight from the heart, not from the brain, while most of the people in her company were accustomed to speaking from their brains. And one of the obstacles getting in the way of his being better understood by his American colleagues was his strong Spanish accent. "How are you with accents, Gail?" Amy asked me. I replied that for the most part, accents were beside the point—but the fact that he spoke from his heart as opposed to his head might give us something very powerful to work with. I wrote a very brief note to myself:

"Part of the problem may also be part of the solution."

My first face-to-face meeting with Andres took place at the company's satellite office in the drab, faceless Boston suburb where his department had been relocated, once again contrary to his expectations of being located in the true corporate headquarters downtown. This big "digital initiative" he had been *designated* to run—but was not actually being *permitted* to run—had been exiled to suburbia, apparently as the result of some Draconian cost-cutting initiative. I have to admit, I had expected to find Andres inhabiting a far more luxurious office environment than the one in which I found him. The Czech author Franz Kafka wrote two harrowing novels, *The Trial* and *The Castle*, based in part on his many years of experience toiling as a mid-level executive in the gigantic Workers' Accident Insurance Institute in Prague. In Kafka's enormous department, junior executives sat in rows of desks arranged on a vast factory floor, while senior executives prowled on corridors suspended above the floor, around the perimeter, gazing down on their subordinates like gods from the heavens.

But let me tell you, the Workers' Accident Insurance Institute in Prague circa 1908 couldn't hold a candle to this monolithic financial services juggernaut circa 2003. I couldn't help but flash on Kafka's predicament as the daring artist caught in the insurance company as I strolled through an aisle of desks to shake hands with Andres. From the moment we met, it was apparent that his forceful and expansive personality simply overflowed the plastic-topped table, identical to dozens of others arranged in rows on a gigantic single floor, behind which he appeared to lose stature. I was seeing the results of a highly touted "open office plan," which had been designed to "facilitate communication" in this post-modern corporate environment. But as the publishing executive Michael Korda once wrote in his 1975 bestseller *Power Places*, "Offices in which management has tried to eliminate the signs and symbols of power to encourage 'openness' are places in which the leadership is determined to retain all the power in its own hands."

It was disturbing to see this proud middle-aged man—whom I could visualize occupying some incredible palatial space in Paris prior to his transfer—now being forced to prowl the hall of this open-plan office, surrounded by a sea of suits. As he stood up to greet me, wearing a beautifully tailored, double-breasted navy blue blazer and open collar, he graciously escorted me to one in a row of conference rooms arranged along one wall. In this confined space, Andres was supposed to open up to me and let it all hang out.

BUILDING ANDRES'S CASTLE

We began as I always begin: by building the castle first. And I didn't mean Kafka's castle. "If you can create something," I asked, "so compelling and so real that it embodies everything that you are passionate about, what would it be? If you can imagine this castle clearly, we can then figure out what we have to do for you to get there without diminishing yourself in the process. It's all about the power of that vision. *How good can we make it?*"

Andres thought about that for a while. What popped into his mind utterly floored me. His private dream castle, he said after taking a deep breath, had nothing whatsoever to do with landing a better, or even the perfect, job at his financial firm, or even a job like the one he had just left, where he had been perfectly happy and fulfilled and content. He then paused. I asked him specifically, "What job would it be that would have you say to yourself, 'I can't believe they're paying me to do this'?"

He thought for a long while before blurting out:

"I'd like to be a journalist back home in Barcelona."

He had always been very close to his mother, he explained, who had been in her youth a well-known stage actress in his native Catalonian capital. His sister, a writer, was also an inspiration to him, and he took his artistic and intellectual side very seriously. He had studied philosophy in college and over the years had written reams of lyric poetry. He was also a big fan of the tango, many of the lyrics of which he knew by heart. He dreamed of one day becoming a writer himself. Becoming a banker and a businessman had been financially and professionally rewarding, he said, but playing the cutthroat game often filled him with ambivalence.

I had been expecting to discuss what he could do to adjust to this new position. I had been expecting to discuss what he might do to communicate better with other people and make a more compelling presentation on the closed-circuit TV screen. And in fact, we did spend a few minutes talking about his habit of slouching and what it meant, and how it affected his ability to step into his own power. But soon after that, to my surprise and delight, we found ourselves talking about Plato and Kant and art and music and the stage. It felt more like a college seminar than a counseling session. Intellectually, we clicked. But I was mindful of my assignment, which involved not only helping him improve his presentation skills, but to avoid becoming, as our mutual friend in human resources had anxiously put it, "a human time bomb."

It was certainly no surprise that Andres had reacted to being dealt such a lousy hand by senior management by becoming "mad as hell" and—as the British actor Peter Finch put it while playing the part of anchorman Howard Beale in the movie *Network*—not being able to take it any more. For much of the time he simply shut down, but when provoked, he exploded. At one staff meeting, he had gotten so bent out of shape that he slammed a fist into a plasterboard wall inches from a colleague's head. It was upon hearing this that I immediately realized that I was looking forward to working with this guy. "At least," I said to myself, "someone who's punching walls still cares about the business." I obviously could not erase the source of his entirely justified frustration. But what I could do was help him channel his restless energy into more positive and productive spheres. It's one thing to become frustrated. It's another thing when that frustration manifests itself in a way that diminishes your capacity to perform.

How did I propose to do all this? Many of us get up five mornings a week and go off to work and come home in the evening without very much happening in between. In the face of this uninspiring environment, many people tend to become resigned and disengaged from their jobs. Andres's situation was simply an exaggeration of an all too common phenomenon. But here's the part of this problem's solution that may seem paradoxical, at first. If we help put these disengaged people in closer touch with their hearts and their wildest dreams—encouraging them to "follow their bliss," as Joseph Campbell so famously put it—this is often the clearest path to more fully reengaging with life. The paradoxical part, I've found, is that people who follow this path not only more fully engage with their highest aspirations, they more fully engage with their work lives as well. What the company needed, what Andres needed, what his colleagues needed, and what his friends and family needed was a man fully engaged with *life*. Perhaps Andres's next trapeze would swing him to Barcelona and a fulfilling new career as a journalist. But just as possibly it would swing him into his new self, the self that embraced all the marvelous possibilities of what it could mean to be Andres—even in his current environment.

A senior executive once expressed a certain amount of anxiety about the end result of my coaching process. "What if you end up encouraging everyone to quit and run off and raise llamas in Peru? Where does that leave me?"

"If people know what they're working for," I replied, "and if they wake up every morning with a renewed sense of purpose, even if that purpose is to work hard until they buy a cottage in the country or a trip to Hawaii, you will get more out of them than if they have no dream and no desire. Realizing that that is their dream, whatever it is, helps them engage more fully in the here and now."

I took a moment to write down a phrase that, to me at least, described Andres's position and his predicament: "The philosopher in the enemy camp."

We took the next step of drawing a circle on a piece of paper. I asked him to imagine that somewhere in that circle were all the limitless possibilities of what it meant to be Andres. There were Andres the poet and Andres the banker and Andres the pirate and Andres the father, husband, brother, and son. I was talking to him about coloring in all the colors in his circle, and we were making eye contact, when out of the blue he gripped my arm and said, very intensely and sincerely, "Gail, I understand now what you are talking about. What you are talking about is what making love is really all about."

"Okay," I said faintly, "let's take a break."

OWNING ANDRES'S GROUND

We began our next session, several weeks later, by talking about owning the ground you've already traveled. "There was a time, wasn't there," I asked, "when you really loved what you were doing? There was a time, wasn't there, when you felt that everything was possible and that there was a great future in store for you?"

He smiled a smile genuinely laced with regret. And then he told me all about his job in Europe, the place where he had shown what he could really do as a businessman, the place where he had truly owned the ground he was walking on. "My objective in life was to run a company. I like running companies. And in that position, I got to run—in a sense—my own company. And with a small unit, you can give your people tools to align their own interests with the company's interests. I particularly enjoyed the management aspect, and I ended up firing my HR person and hiring a new one: myself. I would have people come into my office crying after a negative peer review. I'd say to them, 'Okay, don't cry—you're not being fired. We are going to help you.' And I would help them. No matter what it took, we did it. And you know what? We ended up with record customer satisfaction and employee satisfaction. We managed by motivating and energizing, as opposed to management by fear and coercion. We went from the thirty-fifth bank in the country to number twelve. Customer satisfaction rose from 40 to 70 percent."

While running his own show in Europe, Andres had inspired and motivated a team of people who not only delivered results beyond anything they'd delivered before, but had thoroughly enjoyed themselves in the process. These were people whom he implicitly trusted, and most important, they knew it. Much more important than the spectacular results he had achieved was the way he had achieved them—through love as opposed to fear.

I asked him straight out whether he thought it might be possible to transfer some of that success of the past to his present position. He smiled ruefully and skeptically, and for the first time, an unmistakable tone of resignation crept into his voice. "When a company becomes a parliament, that can be a problem, because you have power centers develop where it is actually possible to block an initiative—by withholding support—not because it isn't good for the company, but because it is not good for the power center."

"You know," I said to him, "you are falling in love with being right about their being wrong."

He stopped and sat straight up in his chair. He wasn't used to being spoken to in that direct way, I suppose. I could tell I had clearly struck a chord in him.

"Could you explain what you mean a little more?" he said, suddenly alert and curious. Now he was no longer the speaker, but the listener. Now he was no longer the teacher, but the student.

ANDRES LETS GO

"It's so *seductive* to be right about their being wrong," I said. I elaborated by asking him how he felt about the fact that his mentor, Alberto, had felt obliged to distance himself from him. I could tell from the look on his face that I had hit a sore spot. We were talking, I knew, about two Spanish gentlemen here, both smart as whips, both given to strutting their stuff and to extravagant gestures, both incredibly successful and accomplished in so many fields, but who, given the right provocation, might well feel compelled to pull out their sabers and duel. I had a sneaking suspicion that Andres's pride had been deeply wounded by Alberto's treatment of him. In this case, he was too proud to tell me about it. Yet I felt that it was important to pry because it was equally important that he not fall prey to the temptation to be right about Alberto's being wrong.

"Could you consider the possibility," I asked, "that Alberto was doing this not to diminish you but to protect you?"

He looked skeptical.

"This is an environment saturated with suspicion and distrust," I said. "It's fostered by the corporate culture. That said, you are—all of you—faced with a number of choices. You can withdraw and eventually implode or disappear." I thought back to a comment that Amy had made, which was that in recent months, a common refrain at the office had been, "Where's Andres?" to which the inevitable reply had been, "Nobody knows."

"But," I continued, "you do have another choice, which is really a very pragmatic choice. In every situation, you get what you expect from people. If you expect them to stab you in the back, they probably will. But if you expect them to take your side and back you up, you may be surprised, because they will probably deliver."

I gave him a homework assignment, for the diligent student I knew he could be.

"I want you to catch at least five people every day doing something *right* today, not something wrong. That is the only way you can get clear of being right about their being wrong. Because that is a trap. It's very seductive, of course, because taken to its logical extreme, that permits you to play the role of the martyr." He laughed in a way that made me know that he heard me. He had been raised a good Catholic, and he knew a little something about martyrdom.

He then broke down to the next layer and began to express the self-loathing he felt about playing, as he put it, "with dirt." By "dirt," he meant that there was a certain amount of moral laxity embedded in the culture of the place, and sometimes whatever he had to do to get ahead made him squeamish. I could practically feel him holding his nose.

"Can you play with dirt without getting some of it on you?" I asked. "My grandmother would have said no without thinking about it."

"My grandmother would have agreed with your grandmother," he laughed.

"But this is here and this is now," I asserted, "and personally, I'm not so sure. I think it's possible to conduct yourself in some of these ambiguous situations with your personal integrity intact. It just takes a little doing. I truly believe that it is possible to live in the sewer and still not be diminished by it."

We talked about the wonderful Italian Holocaust comedy—a very limited genre—*Life Is Beautiful*, in which the character played by Roberto Benigni remains utterly true to his convictions and to himself by finding laughter and beauty even in the moral cesspool of a concentration camp. He has endowed himself with such a strong sense of purpose—to help his son survive—that he *needs* to see the beauty in the ugliness. This becomes his moral imperative.

"Just possibly," I said, "your moral imperative is to see and find the beauty in the ugliness around here, to find the diamond in the lump of coal in other people."

"But it's worse than *The Prince* around here," he protested, referring to Machiavelli. "Look, I can be as selfish and aggressive as the next guy. But what I don't have an easy time doing is BS. I put the truth on the table with such aggressive energy that sometimes people don't know how to react to it. A couple of guys here in my department are absolutely unbelievable; they have no ethics. People lie openly. They say, 'I heard this from so-and-so.' You say, 'But I thought so-and-so said that.' They shrug and say, 'Oh, I guess you're right. What's the difference?' They don't care. They don't think you'll care. So how do you manage them successfully?"

"The challenge," I replied, "lies in not always looking to catch them doing something wrong; catch them doing something right, and let them know it. Sometimes, if you decide to trust people who aren't necessarily inherently trustworthy, they might surprise you. Wouldn't it feel great to be surprised?"

I could tell he was skeptical about that one.

"Our goal," I said, "is for you to be able to express yourself in ways that enable you to move forward and bring everyone else here along with you."

"Today I'm a banker," he replied, "but I'm also a philosopher. Do you know the phrase of Nietszche? 'Even in the act of eating, you are eating yourself up.'"

"Okay," I responded. "You may be telling the truth as you see it, and you say they're too threatened to hear it. But your task, if you want to succeed here, is to tell them the truth in such a way that they do hear it."

He shot me that skeptical look again.

"By telling the truth with humility," I said. "In such a way as to allow for the possibility that you might be wrong, as opposed to the steadfast assurance that you are always right. Only the Pope is supposed to be infallible."

"You know, Gail," he said, "you have mastered the art of helping people see that sensitive, altruistic part of themselves and then helping them to let it come out. But in my business, what is the motivation to do something good for others? Sure, we can say we build companies, but isn't that all just a rationalization? The reality is that we fire people to make these companies run more efficiently, with the social rationalization that an efficiently run company is better for society. But if, as a senior manager, I make one bad decision, that can cost thousands of people their jobs. I may lose my job, too, but the chances are better that they will lose theirs."

I agreed that he was probably right about capitalism and its relentless quest for efficiency, often at the expense of individual livelihoods. But I pointed out that what he had done with his team in Europe was remarkably similar to what we were trying to do together. "Real leadership," I said, "is all about inspiring people to rekindle their passion and apply it to the task at hand."

He smiled at that and said that my point was exceptionally timely, given that he was preparing to meet his newly appointed boss. (Alberto had been transferred and declined to take Andres with him.) He was perfectly willing to admit that his natural inclination would have been to go in there and tell this guy, without preamble, "Okay, here's what you've got to do to make this situation work best for all of us."

I told him, also without preamble, that that was a terrible idea. I relayed an anecdote from my career at Avon, when just before I reached vice-presidential rank I was fortunate—I thought—to find myself seated next to the new boss of my department on a long flight to the Midwest. I seized my opportunity and very carefully laid out for him a stunning vision—or so I thought—of all the wonderful things "we" could do around Avon with his help. I went into some detail and became very emphatic, and at the end of my spiel I saw—to my shock and horror—his face flush and an expression of anger flash into his eyes, before he turned to the window and continued to finish his meal in stony silence.

What had I done to deserve this? I wondered. And immediately, instead of looking for a useful lesson, I became very involved in my being right and his being wrong. It wasn't until many years later, I told Andres, that I opened up John Gray's *Men Are from Mars, Women Are from Venus* and read the following very simple sentence: "Never give a man unsolicited advice."

Andres and I rehearsed a little bit, like a couple of actors. We ran through the opposite approach to his natural bent. We prepared a simple to/from list to help chart out the strategy for the meeting. His instinct was to say to himself, "I know what I know. The point is to let this guy know what I know, and then he'll respect me. And basically, I should have his job anyway."

That was obviously the "from."

The "to" part went something like this:

"If anything were possible, what would you want to have happen around here?"

Then Andres would sit back and listen for as long as it took.

To which his response would be, "I'd like to help you make that happen."

You can be the one, I said, who sparks the ideas of your boss, who, as a result, will love you for it.

Then I reiterated communication lesson number one: *It's not about you; it's about them.* "It's about letting other people know that you trust them," I said, "so that they feel that you are on their side, not just on your side."

Andres was going to meet this man for a drink. Before I left his open office, I made him repeat after me: "I'm so happy to be here. I'm so happy to have a chance to spend a little time with you, to get to know where you'd like this division to go." After the meeting, Andres called me with the good news. It was the first good piece of news I'd heard out of him for a long time.

"It went wonderfully," he said, and I could tell he wasn't trying to fool me, or fool himself. "I think he and I can really work well together. I think we can be part of a team." For Andres, this represented enormous progress, because this was the man who had been given the job Andres felt—with good reason—that he, Andres, deserved. He had come to peace with his situation. He was okay with not knowing how it was all going to turn out. He was ready to . . .

FLY INTO THE VOID

I didn't see Andres for nearly three weeks, as he was traveling all over the world. When we finally got together, he was looking a little bit shaken. Only that morning, he told me, incredulously, he had received an e-mail from his boss, with whom he had been getting along famously, who wrote that he sincerely enjoyed heading up Andres's business unit, but that to his regret, he was being shifted to an entirely different division after a tenure of only forty-five days. Not only that, there was a rumor going around that the viability of Andres's entire operation was now being "reconsidered" at the highest levels.

So what do we do in this predicament? What I suggested to Andres was that rather than sinking into the morass, he step out of it on higher ground. He could with a new sense of detachment put these absurd events on a screen in order to see them more clearly. I was not suggesting that he disengage—detachment is something far more cerebral and emotional. We all needed him to be able to add value to his company while not being ruined by it. In light of his literary aspirations, I suggested that he "cover" the story of himself and his company as if he were a journalist on assignment. His only alternative would be to revel in martyrdom.

The last time I saw Andres, a few weeks before this book went off to press, he came running down the corridor with a big smile on his face, and he gave me a warm bear hug when we finally collided.

"I'm rejoining the firm!" he announced exuberantly, by which I knew that he meant spiritually and metaphysically, since physically he'd never left. I had a feeling after we'd talked for a while that he'd been through a long dark tunnel and finally come out the other end. The strangest thing of all, I can remember myself thinking, is that you hear companies all the time talking about passion and purpose, and here was a guy who had passion in spades and, for the most part, they couldn't figure out what to do with him.

He had recently received a call from a headhunter, he said, with a conspiratorial wink. It involved a very good position in a foreign bank. "You'll never guess where they're based," he laughed. "Madrid. But you know," he said expansively, leaning now *into* instead of *away* from his desk, speaking with passion and purpose and feeling, "I don't really know that I'm ready to leave yet. I've got too much unfinished business around here."

Exercise One: Get What You Expect

On the whole, people really do want to be as good as they think you think they are. So practice giving your children, your spouse, or close friends the impression that you anticipate "good things" from them: that they have good intentions, can be trusted, and will deliver on what they have promised. Write down the good news. Then apply this technique at work. You may be surprised at the results.

Exercise Two: Be Free to Act

Step out of the maelstrom so that you see yourself and your situation more clearly. Play the role of the objective observer, the journalist, the filmmaker, the eyewitness. This is not about pulling away or not participating, but interacting with the situation with a detachment that gives you greater freedom of action. When you are not encumbered emotionally by the all-consuming drama that can pull you to pieces, you can hold yourself at some distance from the edge of the abyss.

Exercise Three: Employ the Andres Love-Making Method

Help people you care a lot about to color in all the colors in their own particular life circles, so that they can see possibilities in themselves and in their daily lives they never could have imagined. You can say, "Hey, what about this? You can start your own business. You can take that trip you've been putting off. You can sign up for that course. Or call that woman who smiled at you on the bus this morning—if only you had asked for her number."

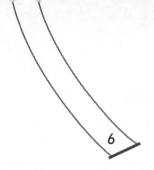

THE PERFECTIONIST

"The true voyage of discovery lies not in seeking
new landscapes, but in having new eyes."
—*Marcel Proust (1871–1922)*

I GAVE A LUNCHEON SPEECH not long ago in Philadelphia, and after the question-and-answer period, a striking-looking young woman with ash blond hair and a fierce, piercing intelligence in her eyes came up to me as I was standing at the podium. She didn't say anything but slipped me a note with her card, then rushed away. The note said, "Gail, I need you to make me a more powerful speaker."

I decided to give Anne Stanton's office number a try, since I was staying over in Philadelphia that night and returning to New York the following afternoon. We agreed to meet at my hotel for breakfast, and she arrived precisely on time, elegantly turned out, ready to get down to business and eager to seize the day.

Practically before she'd sat down and laid a smooth leather briefcase on the seat beside her, she cut straight to the chase. "Gail," she confessed, "I'm really worried. I've just gotten an enormous promotion to become chief marketing officer for my company, and it's going to involve a lot of public speaking and a lot of internal presentations, and I'm really worried I don't come across as a strong enough leader."

We talked casually about the difference between external and internal presentations. Externally you can do the Full Monty. Internally, if you come on as too much of a star, they may end up thinking *you* think it's all about you.

When she told me the name of the company she worked for, I was impressed. If I told you, you'd be impressed too. I could tell from the troubled expression on her face that it had been agony for her to say that she was worried, and that she was—despite her cool, calm, crisp demeanor—genuinely suffering under the surface.

Here was an interesting situation for me. A woman not hoping and dreaming to get something she'd fantasized about all her life, but one who had just gotten her dream job handed to her on a silver platter, feeling as if she'd seen a ghost or a mouse. "You know," I said, taking out a notepad, "you are not alone." She shot me a startled look, which gradually transformed into a wan smile of relief. "In fact," I said, "many people, and in particular women, experience difficulty moving into the next challenge in their lives from their *highest* point. Instead, they instinctively tend to lead from their *lowest* point."

To show her what I was talking about, I drew a diagram composed mainly of a line that peaked and ebbed, like an EKG chart. "People with confidence," I said, "when faced with a challenge, instinctively think back to those defining moments when they faced something like it and got through it with flying colors and were stronger for the struggle." I drew an arrow sticking straight out from a peak, pushing assertively forward. "They lead from the peaks, not from the troughs. But what happens to us when our confidence lags, which happens to just about every one of us at some point, is that, instinctively, we lead from our troughs, not our peaks. What that means, as a practical matter, is that every time we get up to make a speech or a presentation, we assume the worst is going to happen, not the best. We get no extra juice or wind in our sails from all the successful things we've done before."

In times of transition, when we're flying through the air from one trapeze to the next, we all tend to forget under stress that we've pulled it out before and we can pull it out again. "It's so easy to forget," I continued, "when we're one of those electrons making the quantum leap to the next phase that we've done this time and again in our lives.

"I can tell what you're thinking every time you have to make a presentation," I went on. "You're thinking, 'What if this time *they* find out I'm not all that good? What if this time *they* find out I don't know what I'm talking about? And besides, even if I say something great, it doesn't really matter, because they're not going to think it's important.'"

"How did you *know* what I was thinking?"

"Because it's true of all of us," I calmly replied. "I think precisely the same thing myself before I give every speech—before I gave that speech yesterday, if you can believe it. And you want to know something else? Just about *everyone* else is thinking *exactly* the same thing before they do whatever it is they need to do in public. You could be a politician, a college professor, a sales manager, or the head of your local PTA. It's perfectly natural to all of us to be afraid of what 'they' might think, and to assume that what 'they' think is probably negative and that they might be right."

I told her a story that illustrates this problem, which is really a problem of fact versus interpretation. I once gave a speech to a group of executives at Texaco, and after I was done, the woman who had brought me in walked me to the elevator, since I was rushing off to catch a plane. As we were saying goodbye, she said, "Gail, there's one thing I've got to talk to you about before you leave. When we were having lunch today, I noticed that you were looking at me really, really hard. And Gail, *I knew what you were thinking*," she said triumphantly.

I must have looked a little bit puzzled, because she delivered her own punch line. "You were thinking, 'Her makeup's all wrong.'"

Trying to keep a straight face, I said, "What you were seeing, actually, was me listening. I was so riveted by what you were saying, I was just trying really hard to absorb everything you were saying."

She looked skeptical, to say the least, and wouldn't let me into the elevator before extracting a promise to send her some pointers about improving her cosmetics. She knew, of course, that I'd been a senior executive at Avon and assumed I was an expert in makeup in addition to makeovers.

"The reason we're all terrified," I told Anne over breakfast in Philadelphia, "about public speaking and about presenting ourselves in public is that we're all a little like that woman at Texaco. We think it's all about us. We think that we're constantly being judged, graded, decided upon by others. But once you realize that they're far more likely to be thinking about *themselves*, it all gets much, much easier to handle. *It's not about you, it's about them.* Once you shift your attention from yourself—"How am I doing? Do they like me?"—to *them*—"How are they doing? Are they getting what they need?"—the terror will dissipate, and you will begin to step into your own power."

She still looked a little bit lost, so I pointed out, "Look, Anne, what are you going to do, *let someone else do this job?*"

That one sat her straight up in her feet, and made her lovely eyes flash like daggers in the light. No, she was not about to do that! I'd struck a hard chord somewhere inside her, something defiant and flinty, and it was easy to see why this enormous public company had put such trust in her to run this critical function at this critical time—not that every time isn't a critical time. She had grit and determination, talent and drive and intelligence. She was a classic example of Franklin Roosevelt's dictum that sometimes the only thing we have to fear is fear itself.

"But what about my media training?" she plaintively asked. "What about telling me how to hold my hands and not to wave too much and what to wear and all that? I came to you so you could help me make stronger speeches!"

"We'll take care of all that," I said, "or I guess I'd better say, if we do this job right, it is going to take care of itself."

If we did the job right, I insisted, her body was going to *know* how to perfectly reflect her passion and her soul. Because all strong speeches, I reiterated, come from the inside and really have very little to do with not waving your arms or speaking in a particular intonation or cadence. "We're going to be working on your heart, not your mind. When the heart speaks, the world will hear you."

Before rushing off to her first morning meeting, she silently slipped a slim manila envelope toward me. I slid a few neatly typed onionskin pages out of the envelope, which were labeled "Review: Anne Stanton." As I skimmed through her résumé and biography, I began to think a bit about why, right off the bat, I had taken such a shine to her. She was spunky and lovely, smart and honest and—although she didn't know it yet—really quite brave.

Anne's peer review sheet was a surprising document for anyone disposed to take a dim view of large impersonal companies, which one typically assumes would never take the time or trouble to really understand individual employees and their problems and issues. But if they have the resources and the commitment and the will—and enough investment in you—a big company can do just about anything, including paying someone very well to understand you. Anne was, in a very real sense, in precisely the opposite position from Andres, who was highly talented and self-assured, but had been stuck in a dreadful spot. Anne was equally talented, if somewhat less self-assured. But in her case, the company had gone out on a limb to put her in the perfect spot for her to grow—they were challenging her to lift herself to the next step. Her challenge was not to get the right spot. Her challenge was to own it.

The review was sensitively written and carefully thought through. The executive summary described a highly competent woman who is "bright, creative, and driven and loves facing up to a challenge." It also said, right up front, "she plays to win." She had grown up in the Southwest, in a family of fairly strict Baptists. These were not people who put a whole lot of stock in having fun, kicking back, mellowing out, or smelling the flowers. Which was great, insofar as it went, in that this strict upbringing, combined with loads of natural creative ability and an unusually high level of executive skills, made her a formidable professional competitor. "She can have the ideas and drive them through to a successful conclusion," her anonymous assessor wrote, approvingly. This was why they were promoting her to the big leagues. I wrote a note to myself: "It might be a good idea if Anne rented the film *Bull Durham* and absorbed the lessons learned by Kevin Costner," who plays a longtime minor league player who makes it to the majors, while absorbing a number of hard-to-learn lessons about life.

Anne had also, at a very young age, accomplished great things. She had consistently brought new concepts to market and seen complex projects through to fruition. But now, as her evaluation plainly stated, there was a rub. In her new corporate role, she needed to fundamentally expand in a few areas, as opposed to superficially. There is a moment in your career when it is simply no longer good enough to be good. It's no longer enough just to be brilliant at delivering results. When you climb to a certain level, the job requirements involve less tangible, more personal and interpersonal skills.

We're really talking about an arena that few of us are truly prepared for, by our educations or early job experiences. We learn skills on the job, but even when we are highly competent—often *particularly* if we are highly competent—we get by on results. It's the opposite of really smart people who don't seem to work hard and coast on their intelligence. This is about really bright people who also work really hard and pay their dues, but miss out on something else in their evolution—the human factors.

A number of funny new things can happen to you on your way

to a "C-level" job—the "C" here signifying "chief," as in chief executive officer, chief financial office, or chief marketing officer, which was Anne's new and terrifying title. Clearly, you can't deliver less good results; if anything, the pressure to deliver concrete results becomes even more intense. But at these loftier levels, the need to step back and take a broader view becomes an integral part of the job. One area of potential improvement was in dealing with her peers and her one superior, the CEO. Before every meeting with her CEO, I advised Anne to step back and think long and hard about what he was threatened by and what he was looking for, in both the short and long terms. In particular, I advised her to pay close attention to what was going on with her peer group—now a very small group, clustered at the very top of the pyramid—so that she wouldn't be blindsided by developments that arose purely from group dynamics.

One of the disadvantages of being so wonderfully competent and results driven for all her life was that she had largely missed out on having to lead, motivate, and inspire other people to create great results themselves. She was so impressive she almost didn't need other people. The fact that motivating others wasn't necessarily her strong suit had not so far proved an impediment to her advancement. But at the same time, it had not gone unnoticed that some of the people who worked for her tended to be so intimidated by her that they didn't know quite where to start when trying to please her. She could be incredibly impatient in dealing with subordinates' mistakes—or what she perceived as mistakes—and she could be incredibly impatient with people who didn't "share her pace" and drive to succeed. If someone in her department wasn't running on all six cylinders all of the time, she didn't get it. She thought of them as slackers. Her typical response to someone not functioning at the level of performance she did was to simply take the job over herself, to get it done, to get the results she demanded, to get the product out the door. She was the perennial good student determined to get nothing less than an A. From Anne's point of view, it didn't matter who did it, as long as it got done. But from her subordinates' point of view, it mattered very much. As a result, she could come off as aloof, high-handed, and unwilling to delegate appropriately, or at least not enthusiastically. She wasn't exactly great at saying thank you or giving credit, either. It's not that she didn't care about it—it's just that she was so eager to get on to tackling the next task that she simply never got around to it.

THE UNIMPORTANCE OF BEING PERFECT

Think of the business person who makes all the right moves and goes to the right schools and takes all the right risks, or no risks, and ends up in all the right jobs, until she or he ends up in the right nursing home before heading for the right graveyard.

Think of the perfect hostess who knows all the right things to say to all the right people who think the right thoughts and share all the right prejudices. The narrow idea of what constitutes success is something that we tend to buy into, which leaves us very vulnerable to despair when and if someone ever pulls the plug on us.

There is a common term for people like this. They are known as perfectionists. Taken to a certain degree of moderation—although by definition, this is hard to do—perfectionism can be a positive trait. Most of the world's top film directors, art directors, museum directors, and financial and corporate directors tend to be perfectionists, and they pride themselves on their perfectionism. I am a bit of a perfectionist myself, and I recognized the trait immediately in Anne. But it can also be a dangerous trait, because it can suck a lot of fun and joy out of life. The true perfectionist is never satisfied, never content, either with her own performance, or with others'.

Anne had grown up, as many of us do, believing that if she didn't explicitly please her parents, that they wouldn't respect her or love her. She, like many of us, had grown up with high expectations, expectations of being just about perfect. Now, she had to learn to abandon that perfectionist approach in dealing with her own peers and subordinates, her own children and loved ones, and—above all—herself. Because one very real problem with perfectionism is that the main victims aren't only the people whom perfectionists feels compelled to hold up to their exacting standards. The perfectionist's primary victim is often herself.

When our daughter Kate was still little and our daughter Abigail had not yet been born, every morning before work I would take Kate to a little nursery school in our neighborhood. I would dread running into all the other mothers in their casual clothes, because I would be in my corporate suit carrying my briefcase and feeling terribly guilty about not being the one who would be picking her up later.

I would always see a woman there whom I began to refer to as "the perfect mother." I knew she would pick up her perfect little boy and take him to the park for perfect little picnics. Her family photo albums, I also knew, were all perfectly updated and labeled with every year in perfect gold leaf. Our family photograph, representing years and years of family vacations and "priceless moments," are right now stuffed into at least five drawers.

All I wanted was to be like her. I was *dying* to be like her. I wanted her perfect, wonderful life. I wanted the serenity, the tidiness. It would never have occurred to me that it was perfectly plausible that she considered me the perfect woman—and I had no reason to think that she didn't.

The quest for perfection can be paralyzing. One of my college roommates was an excellent artist. She knew so much about classical music and art, and I was very impressed by her. One weekend her mother came to visit, and she proudly showed her mother her latest painting. "Well, it's pretty good," her mother said, "but you'll never be Renoir." My roommate put down her paint brushes and never picked them up again. She, you see, wasn't perfect. She had absorbed this dangerous notion—I had a pretty fair idea of who from—that if she couldn't be Renoir, what was the point? You may remember that Peter Mazza had pretty much concluded before coming to see me that if he weren't good enough to win the Thelonious Monk competition, what was the point? Being a semi-finalist wasn't good enough. We all pay a very high price for our obsession with perfection and our need for approval. We douse our own fires so that no one else has to.

So here we had a portrait of a perfectionist at a crossroads. The main issue with perfectionists is that in the midst of their brilliance and their achievement, there is often a missing ingre-dient: trust—by which I mean trust in other people, as well as trust in ourselves. This trust also involves trusting our instincts to identify the right people to be part of our team and then trusting them to do the very best job that they can. Anne's skills, which were really quite stunning, as stunning as she was, had brought her this far—very far. But in order to make it to the next level, to grasp her next trapeze, to fly into her next great life, she was going to have to evolve into a more multidimensional per-sonality. She was going to have to take a leap from her old trapeze of obsessive perfectionism into the vast unknown of pos-sible imperfection. She had to let go of that part of herself and let others work not only *for* her, but *with* her. She could no longer just perform on one level; she could no longer simply keep her eyes on the immediate prize and the task ahead in just the short term. She would have to shift her focus away from pure task orientation to a more long-term strategic view, encompassing not just concrete "deliverables," but also the more complex interactions between people at the top. As the chief marketing officer, she had to take the CEO's broad vision and fill in the brushstrokes; and she had to be capable of projecting and communicating this vision clearly both internally and externally.

The note I wrote to myself after reading Anne's corporate "life story" was this:

> Anne knows if she works really, really hard she can get incredible results. But in some sense, that is *all* she knows about herself. She doesn't have an easy time acknowledging the contribution of the people who work for her. She doesn't easily delegate. She will need to believe that with a different approach she can get the same or even better results.

Shortly after our next session, Anne was preparing to have what you might call a power lunch with one of the heads of the business units, whose overarching fear was that the power and control he exercised over his unit would be directly threatened by her role as the great integrator of all the business units. As chief marketing officer, one of her jobs was to bring the units into alignment as part of the corporate brand. This was a not uncommon occurrence at big companies, in my experience, because at the same time that they like to give all sorts of decentralized power to the heads of the business units, they also want someone in the head office to preside over the whole smorgasbord as the sacred keeper of the brand.

This man sensed her vulnerability, Anne suspected, and intended to play on it for all it was worth, if she let him. Anne knew what he was up to and was not about to let him get away with it. Now, her typical "old self" response to that sort of game would have been, "Okay buster, I'm going to *show* you." And what she meant by that was that she intended to deliver results, doggedly, determinedly, even grimly, even if it killed her. She was going to show him; she was going to show *them*. What I tried to show *her*, though, was that that response might be perfectly appropriate to the lower and even the middle echelons, but that when it came to playing in the big leagues, she needed to have a clearer sense of both what other people around her were trying to accomplish and how she could help them—at every level— realize those goals.

I tried to persuade her that she should take this guy out to lunch, that she should call him first, offer the invitation, make sure to pick up the tab. But in the beginning, she resisted. She wasn't one of those people who particularly liked doing business over lunch. Again, this excessive compartmentalization had served her well in the past. But in her new incarnation, this same old way of thinking and being could prove a self-laid landmine.

These business units—reflecting the decentralized nature of the company—are spread out across many different office buildings in downtown Philadelphia. I suggested that she say, "Next time I'm near your office, let's have lunch." She looked shocked. It would behoove her to be bold, to be forward, to even catch him a little off guard, I said. And once she had him right where she wanted him—she would pick the restaurant, and the time to meet—she was going to *surprise* him. How? She would not just pretend to listen. She really *would* listen.

This was a classic turf battle—or rather, would become one, if she let it fester into one. But she had an opportunity to cut off all that unpleasantness at the pass by stopping and thinking about what this other guy was actually trying to accomplish and what his fears and dreams might be. He was threatened by her marketing function because it required these disparate business units to all pull together, while what he really wanted was to be left along to steer his own ship—a perfectly natural and human desire.

But if she approached this situation a different way, the tension between them could be removed. Rather than making it all about her being right and his being wrong, she could first find out from him what he was really hoping to have happen, in the broadest sense, and then, after listening to him carefully, explain how her vision could help bring his into focus. And at the end of that conversation, he might even end up thinking to himself, "You know, I was wrong about her. Maybe she isn't out to simply reduce my autonomy and authority." And then, just possibly, an opportunity would present itself for them both to relax. This, I strongly suggested, was what team-building and leadership was all about, not jousting and besting others in turf battles or controlling people or processes, but inspiring people with your vision—and being inspired by theirs.

So she called him. And he was perfectly cordial. They had lunch. Afterward, he sent an e-mail: "I think you're really terrific, and I appreciate what you're trying to do here." Afterward, she sent me an e-mail. She was very proud of herself. "I think I came across as a good facilitator," she said in her note. What mattered here was that she had taken the initiative and won this guy over; she had been warm and engaging and not aloof. The next time I saw her, she couldn't stop expressing her surprise at how well this technique had worked. "I concentrated on finding out what's important to him," she said, "and I discovered what he's trying to achieve in his unit."

"That way," I replied, "without saying anything, he's found out what you are trying to achieve. Which is mending fences and bringing these disparate fiefdoms into alignment." I was as proud of her as she was of herself. One thing you can say about Anne—she really is a quick study.

It can be such a relief, I told her, when you decide that it's really all about them, not about you. Leadership is really about putting everyone *else's* best feet forward. Whether you're leading a cavalry charge or running a company, a country, a political campaign, or a division of a company, it doesn't matter. If someone on your team messes up, you don't always have to take it so personally. Of course, we are responsible for what our teams do, but that doesn't mean that all their deficiencies and inefficiencies are yours. That realization can give you room to be generous to other people, because if you don't feel so personally responsible for them, you won't feel so personally beholden to them.

Anne and I ran through some adjectives that described her old self, the one she'd like to shed like a snake's skin. We came up with *harsh, aloof, remote.* We also worked on some adjectives for her new self: *Confident. Delightful. Engaging. Embracing. Warm. Vulnerable. Enabling. Celebrating Other People.*

That is what we call a true metamorphosis. Her "From/To" list went as follows:

1. From *doing it all by yourself* to *enabling others to do it.*

2. From *being the shy type* to *being the engaging type.*

3. From *being all business* to *cracking other people up.*

4. From *getting results* to *stirring and inspiring others to create.*

5. From *fear of being criticized* to *I can be controversial.*

Anne's great aim in life has always been to show the world how *good* she is. In her late thirties, she remains the quintessential good girl. I know the drill, because I am very much that way myself. But in her present position, the way she would have to be good was to show the world *how good her people were.* To keep being good on her own just wasn't good enough anymore. Now she had to actively look for ways to positively reinforce her people. Making people feel good about themselves had to be high on her priority list. Very simply, she had to go from making people feel bad about themselves in her presence to making them feel good about themselves in her presence. *And one of the things she very much had to let go of was desperately needing everyone else's approval.*

When I was a little girl, I went to a birthday party and came home crying my eyes out. When my mother asked me why I was crying, I said through my tears, "Because Suzy Wright doesn't like me."

I'll never forget what my mother said next. I think of these words all the time.

"Gail, darling, can you think of anything that absolutely *everybody* likes? I can think of only one thing—*water*. And that's because it has no taste. Do you want to be like water?"

If you don't desire a life of quiet desperation, you have to stop worrying about not rocking the boat. If you want to be able to say to yourself when you're eighty, "I wouldn't have missed that life of mine for anything," you have to be able to let go of the desire to be so invisible they can never notice you and fire you. In the process of following that tidy path you risk losing yourself. Your real self.

I told Anne right up front that if she wanted to succeed at this new job, not only was she going to have to let go of the perfectly natural desire for everyone to like her, to approve of her, to give her an A. She was going to have to let herself be controversial.

"You know," I said, "in the end, every organization is nothing more—or less—than a collection of people, people who either do or don't find themselves motivated, inspired, or valued by their leaders. All those goals, targets, aspirations, and missions have to be set by leaders who have to know how to galvanize people to want to do their personal best. If you're going to be a powerful and effective leader, you're going to have to do and say things that shake up old assumptions and challenge the conventional wisdom. One way to inspire people is to take them by the hand and gently lead them out of their comfort zones so that they can discover new possibilities and own them."

This thought led directly to her next dilemma, her upcoming meeting with her boss, the CEO. We role-played the scenario. "Your objective for this meeting," I said, "and indeed for every meeting with him, is that he comes away from the conversation convinced that if there's one person out there whom he can really trust, who really gets it about what he's trying to accomplish, it's you."

Her old way of handling these situations would have been to

walk in, hand him what she considered a great new idea, and ask for his immediate approval. I knew about this one from extensive personal experience. But the problem with that approach is that it's too easy for the recipient of these great ideas, particularly if that person has a hefty ego and a lot at stake, to feel as if something is being shoved down his throat. His natural reaction to such an approach could easily have been that her suggestion was an implied criticism of his performance. On a prior occasion, she had tried this method and encountered resistance. His response was to simply shut down and observe with irritation, "Let's not push the panic button here."

This idea of shifting approaches initially made her a little nervous. At first blush, she took my suggestion to mean that she should be fabricating something artificial or pandering to his ego. "But I've got no patience with BS and hypocrisy," she protested. She felt uncomfortable "playing an act."

"It's got to be authentic," I replied. "As with any audience, they always know when it's not. Your challenge is to find where your vision authentically connects with his."

Building the Castle for Anne involved elevating the role of marketing in her company so that it formed the context in which all of these wildly spinning satellites could be brought into regular and orderly orbits around a common sun—the brand. Her vision involved creating genuine synergy, that often overused term that is more easily generated in mission statements and speeches than in practice. The CEO's vision was, of course, very much in alignment with this. But her aspiration was to make her particular function inspire that feeling of unity—and reality of cooperation—that was truly their common goal.

As part of reinforcing that broad corporate vision, Anne was preparing to deliver a major speech, which we spent some time working on together. Although the audience wasn't to know it, this was going to be the big inaugural speech in which she introduced her new self to them. "The exact words you say are almost incidental right now," I started out. She looked a little bit baffled. "What matters most is transmitting your enthusiasm about the future of the company and how marketing can help them create new opportunities for their business units. What matters here is that you pose the question, 'How good can we make it together?' and that you start encouraging them to ask and answer it for themselves.

"This is where you want to *let these people know that you think they're exactly the right people to lead this enterprise forward.* What you want to bring to this meeting is your infectious energy and enthusiasm and your conviction that this is going to be *as good as it gets.* Have fun with this one—and that will give it the pizzazz, the fizz, the buzz that it needs."

She gave her speech. And it went fabulously. She was terrific. I know because a day or so after she gave it, she sent me a tape of her performance for my critique. The transformation was truly astonishing. She was so strong and so sure of herself that even when she was speaking, she appeared to be listening. She connected so well with her audience that she drew her energy from them, as well as from inside herself—or rather, from the electric connection between them. She sparkled, she was funny, she told stories, she was spontaneous. This was everything but your typical power-point, bulleted list of goals and accomplishments, missions and targets. She had discovered her own voice, and I was truly proud of her.

When I spoke to her about it later on, I was happy to hear her sounding so upbeat. Someone in the audience had told her after her speech, "Wow, you've really taken off. Your public speaking is really improving."

The old Anne would have thought to herself, "What did that person *really* mean? That I was really terrible before? Was I terrible? I probably was. He's not saying that I'm actually good, he's just saying that I'm not as bad I used to be."

The new Anne simply said, "I really appreciate that."

I asked her, point blank, to grade herself on her performance. We were both surprised when she said, with a grin, "Well, it wasn't perfect, but I'd give myself an A."

Exercise One: Be the One

Always lead from your highest point, not your lowest. Who could possibly be better than you at doing this job? Starting this company? Making this speech? Marrying this person? Do it—

whatever it is—for the sheer joy of it, not for the rightness of it or for doing it perfectly. For the longest time, even Renoir didn't think he was "Renoir."

Exercise Two: Take a Look at Midnight

What's the worst thing that can happen to you in any given situation? At work, it would be getting fired, right? Many, if not most, highly accomplished people get fired, from time to time. People who are most "like water"—that is, deliberately bland—tend to survive, but never thrive. For some trapeze artists, *not* getting fired would be something to worry about. Trapeze artists never confuse falling with failing. The greatest flyers are always the greatest fallers. Imagine yourself taking a big risk, and then very concretely determine the worst case scenario. As inspirational author Larry Wilson—a mentor of mine—often used to remind me, "What's the worst thing that can happen? Will the world actually come to an end? Will you actually die? No. Is it inconvenient? Yes. Does it make it not worth doing? No."

7

THE DRIVER

IT WAS OCTOBER 2002 and Family Weekend at Skidmore College in Saratoga, New York, where our younger daughter, Abigail, was just beginning her sophomore year. The college administration had arranged for a few interested parents to talk to the students about their careers—or, as authority figures always put it in this day and age, "career options." The setup was informal and non-threatening: a nice large room comfortably furnished with tables and chairs. Any students who cared to do so were sitting around chatting with parents in this low-pressure atmosphere, and, as low key as it might have been, it didn't stop a significant proportion of these students from feeling a fair amount of pressure—to get their lives in order, to nail down a career, to get a direct bead on the future.

Then an exceptionally bright, attractive, and poised young

woman stepped up to ask me a question or two. This obviously capable young lady was concerned about choosing a major, not so much because she wasn't quite sure what she wanted to do academically, but because she felt unsettled about the possibility that whatever major she ultimately chose might not directly lead to a brilliant and stable career.

Karen Smyth was a freshman and contemplating majors in English and music. Skidmore's superb music department was one of the reasons she had chosen to stray so far from her native Texas. As best I could, I tried to give her my personal perspective on this issue, which was that there are certain rare points in your life when you are fortunate to find yourself not having the faintest idea of what the future might bring. You should value these times, I suggested, as opposed to dreading, rejecting, or ignoring them. "It's okay *not* to know how it's all going to work out," I insisted. "In fact, it can be *great* not to know. These 'not knowing' times present opportunities to open yourself up to an infinite array of new possibilities. These are the times when *you* get to decide, and when *you* get to create a new self—any self that you want to create, without limits."

Karen asked me to elaborate a bit, if I could, because she found that what I was saying carried quite a different message from what she was absorbing from the surrounding culture. Despite the message at Skidmore, where the slogan is CREATIVE THOUGHT MATTERS, and the fact that the institution goes out of its way to stress adventure and openness, the larger cultural atmosphere

was negatively saturated with urgent imperatives to nail everything down, to figure everything out, to have everything planned
out strategically, so that you wouldn't stumble on any rung of
your safe, stable ladder straight to the top.

I said that as far as I was concerned, and based on my own experience, a lot of these conventional concepts—stability, security,
a safe approach—were nothing but reassuring illusions. In
today's high-risk, low-security world, I told Karen, the pursuit of
security and of certain knowledge is a chimera, and often a dan-
gerously narrowing one at that. Because when the rug does get
pulled out from under us—as it inevitably will at some point in
our careers—we often find ourselves woefully unprepared to respond effectively. I compared today's world to a ship at sea,
rocked and buffeted by currents beyond all our controls. A good
sailor develops "sea legs," which means that he or she can react
fluidly and flexibly to the rolling swells, more like an expert
surfer than an immovable brick wall. This profound social shift
meant that the acquired skill to ride the waves (and enjoy the
sheer thrill of it) was just as important a capacity for somebody
in mid-career as it was for a college freshman.

Before I was through, I had given this curious young woman a
spirited, if brief, defense of the underlying premise of the tradi-
tional liberal arts education. Education at its best, I said, is a
voyage of continual discovery into the unknown, more like
Columbus piloting the Pinta across the Atlantic than today's
yachtsman cruising the coastal waters with his Global Posi-

tioning System, supplemented by short wave radio and the Coast Guard. The greatest value of education is that it enables you to form a *habit* of discovery, a *habit* of learning, a *habit* of opening up to new possibilities, despite the fears that we all share in confronting the unknown.

"Take risks when you can," I advised Karen Smyth. "This is a time of true freedom. Your only responsibility is to explore. It's a time for discovering what you're passionate about. Of course, eventually you will hone in on a major, but that major doesn't need to have any direct connection to what you do later in life."

As I observed this thoughtful young woman, only a year younger than our own daughter, pondering her major and the meaning of life, I became vaguely aware that someone else was standing quietly on the periphery of our conversation, listening intently to every word we were saying without saying a word himself. Catching sight of an attractive man with distinguished salt-and-pepper hair who I would have guessed to be in his mid-fifties, Karen introduced me with a shy smile to her father, Jack Smyth.

"You know," Jack said politely, at first hesitant to intrude upon our conversation, "I couldn't help being intrigued by what you've been saying, because the more I thought about it, the more I honestly began to think that it might apply to my situation as well as to my daughter's." I asked Jack to take a few minutes, if he would, to fill me in on his story. Apart from the specifics, the broad brushstrokes were depressingly familiar to many of us in this era of callous corporate consolidation and ruthless industry shakeouts. Jack's story was—and is—the embodiment of the classic and, unfortunately, not uncommon story of the highly regarded, highly successful upper-middle-level corporate executive who has performed his job every day for year after year not just with competence or engagement, but with exemplary devotion, commitment, skill, and pride. Jack is the kind of guy who wouldn't know how to do a bad or indifferent or incomplete or uninspired job if you asked him to. He had spent seven years working hard for a company he loved—Compaq— before it was acquired by another company—Hewlett-Packard.

Compaq had promoted, valued, and rewarded him year after year with favorable performance reviews, annual bonuses and raises, exciting new possibilities, and opportunities to grow in his career. So it came as a bit of a shock when—as he expressed it to me without rancor or bitterness—he found himself "blown out of Compaq/HP" when the ax fell on 20,000 employees in the fall of 2002, only a few weeks before Family Weekend at Skidmore. He related this event matter-of-factly, with a wry smile that obviously masked a good deal of pain and suffering under a posture of relentless optimism. That he was holding up, so far, pretty well under the pressure was a testament to his character, which I would describe as quintessentially Western American. He was the don't-wallow-in-the-muck type, the let's-pick-ourselves-up-when-we-get-knocked-down type, the don't-cry-over-spilled-milk kind of guy. Might he have been frightened, anxious, unsure of himself in a way that he had never known before? If I'd had to bet, I would have said that he was doing an excellent job of putting the best face on what was an objectively bad situation.

Karen had mentioned that she had an older sister who was attending college, too. Pretty early on in our conversation, I learned that her twin was also intending to start college in the near future. Jack was clearly carrying those and many other burdens into a future no less uncertain than that of his college-age daughters. His most recent assignment at Compaq, Jack told me, just as it was merging with HP, had been to increase service sales through Compaq's telemarketing centers in the United States and Canada, from which more than eight hundred telesales reps sold hardware to customers every day. After eight months under Jack's supervision, service sales through these telemarketing sessions rose over 500 percent to more than three hundred million dollars, on an annualized basis. In accepting this position—in anticipation of the merger—he had deliberately shifted from a staff position into a sales position, where compensation was linked more to commission than salary, in the hope of finding a safe haven in what he could easily foresee would be a tumultuous and uncertain environment.

Shortly after Compaq's merger with HP, the joint workforce was informed that some twenty thousand jobs would be eliminated. Jack had initially assumed that his job was comparatively safe. Many of us cherish an illusion of indispensability, and Jack Smyth was no exception. He had done so well at his job, at all of his jobs. His skills had been widely recognized, and he had won so many internal awards for the excellence of his presentations to major customers—Jack was the first recipient of Compaq's Speaker Recognition Award for "Positive Influence on Our Customers' Experience"—that when he got the pink slip, he was shocked senseless. As Jack put it, "After the layoffs came down, the rationale they presented to me was, 'Hey, you've built up this organization and gotten it up and running, so we really don't need you anymore.'

"I was getting pretty well paid," Jack said, almost apologetically, "so I guess you could say that when push came to shove, I was a budget-cutter's dream." It was also obviously the case that he was not going to be an easy hire because of his age, his seniority, his wealth of experience, and the pay scale that typically went with that talent base. Most companies in his industry, in the interests of remaining "competitive," were looking to hire two or three folks just getting started for the price they would have paid for one Jack Smyth, who was just ten years from retirement age.

"Jack," I said, hoping that this wouldn't sound too presumptuous, given that we'd only just met, "you know, it's actually possible that one day soon, you might end up feeling grateful to your friends at HP for doing you the favor of blowing you right off your old trapeze and forcing you to take a deep breath, to look around, to *look inside* for what may be your next step."

I really took a shine to Jack Smyth right away, in part because

I liked his reaction to what I was saying, which could easily have been dismissed by many a hyper-rational executive as off-the-wall "soft" stuff. As opposed to looking in the least bit defensive or baffled or skeptical, he leaned forward and, with a sincerely positive tone in his voice, asked curiously, "Really? How do you see that?"

"The reason that you might find your next step inside, as opposed to outside," I went on, encouraged by his response, "is that you may have been keeping a dream inside you that now you have this tremendous opportunity to release. And now, thanks to your friends at HP, you can act on and realize that dream with a level of commitment that you never could have brought to bear if it had just been a weekend thing, or a hobby. You know, right now, the only questions that really matter in your life are, 'How good can I make it? What is my dream? What am I *really* dying to do?'"

I told him the story of Walt Disney and building the castle, and as our conversation continued and deepened, we were joined by his wife, Linn. We talked about the idea that the best way to figure out what your dream is is to think of the last time that you really felt great about what you were doing. His eyes lit up, and after shooting a quick glance at his wife, he told me the story of how, recently, he had discovered his passion.

Two and a half years before, he had purchased a Honda S 2000 sportscar and enthusiastically plunged into autocross racing, a medium-speed event in which a driver negotiates a course laid out with traffic cones in a parking lot; vehicles run against the clock, not wheel-to-wheel. Autocross racing is not about speed, but about control. He had found it gratifying to discover within himself this sense of power and mastery he felt just from knowing how to control this high-performance machine in all sorts of high-pressure, high-stakes (if not always high-risk) situations. Autocross racing, Jack assured me, was not a form of thrill seeking based on *taking* risk, but on *controlling* risk. What had started out as a fun weekend hobby rapidly accelerated into a serious passion for Jack. After becoming an active participant in regularly scheduled autocross events sponsored by both the BMW and Porsche clubs of Houston, he soon qualified as an instructor. As he became more involved, he began to think seriously about establishing some sort of school that would expand upon basic car control physics and apply it to general driver's education.

As Jack spoke about his dream with mounting passion and optimism, I began to find his vision personally infectious. It was sheer coincidence that my husband, Jim, and I had over the years become friendly with the great race car driver Skip Barber and his wife, Judy, who, like Jack's wife, happens to be an interior designer (she helped us refurbish our old farm house in Connecticut). We had enrolled both our daughters when they were teenagers in the well-known Skip Barber Driving School. Both Kate and Abigail had learned an enormous amount from the course, and Jim and I have often remarked since that we consider it one of the best investments we've ever made.

Before we said goodbye and went our separate ways, Jack and I agreed that we would work together, by e-mail, fax, and phone. During our first telephone session, shortly thereafter, I explained my belief that we would need to work on parallel tracks. On Track One, he needed to land a new position with an appropriate income. On Track Two, he needed to follow his dream and his passion to wherever it might lead him, ideally to fruition, satisfaction, and possibly even profit. His "dream" track could provide an incalculable amount of energy to his "security" track. If he gave both of them equal time, he would end up building not one castle, but two: one in the foreground, the other in the background. We talked about the essential difference between "urgent" and "important." Finding a new job was urgent; following his true passion was *important*.

As part of his severance package, Jack had been given six months of outplacement services. He applied himself rigorously to the job of getting a job. He became part of a work team, which met every Monday from ten to twelve, when every member was expected to openly describe their successes and failures of the prior week, the leads they had developed, the contacts they had made, the networking they had engaged in, their hot prospects and their cold prospects, and their thoughts for the immediate future. Jack relished "the peer pressure," as he put it, and found that he left these sessions invigorated, optimistic, ready to seize the day and the week. He also found that taking the standard psychological, personality, and skill evaluations like

Myers-Briggs was useful to him in homing in on his true interests and obvious skills. "When it came to determining my natural skills and interests, all the tests overwhelmingly showed that my great interest was driving and my skills involved teaching and training."

When we talked about building his corporate castle, not in the sky but resting firmly on the ground, we focused on those moments when he had really felt good about what he was doing, when he felt, "I can't believe they're actually *paying* me to do this." He recalled some moments vividly. During all his years at Compaq, he had most enjoyed giving the "corporate overview" to key customers and major accounts like Shell Oil, JPMorgan Chase, and SBC Corp. He discovered that he enjoyed these personal interactions so much that these presentations evolved into an art form of sorts—performance pieces, if you will.

As for his entrepreneurial castle, that began to materialize far sooner than he might have foreseen. Not long after we met, Carol Hymowitz, who writes a regular column about careers for the *Wall Street Journal*, became interested in the plight of the newly unemployed in an unusually weak job market. She called me for a general view on what people in this unfortunate position might do to get a fresh start in life. I suggested that people could value these "between trapezes" periods and actually turn them to their benefit. Thinking of the advice I had just given to Karen—as well as Jack—I said to Carol, "Being between trapezes is a time to find out who you are, at least for now, and what talent you have forgotten or are just discovering in yourself."

I suggested that she call up Jack Smyth for a view from the trenches. Jack was extremely open with Carol and found to his delight that his dream of starting a sophisticated twenty-first-century driver's ed course became the core of Carol's piece in the *Journal*. Several months later, as the result—appropriately enough—of taking a long drive with his wife, Jack's entrepreneurial castle began to take even clearer shape. "Linn and I were just driving back to Texas from her mother's funeral in North Carolina," he told me a couple of days later. "We got to talking about our teenage daughters." Like all parents of teenagers, he and his wife were anxious about their daughters' driving. It wasn't that they were bad drivers, but that for perfectly obvious and natural reasons they were not as experienced as drivers with years more time on the road and behind the wheel.

Like many parents, he and his wife had been less than impressed by the level of skill preparation and real-life simulation of conditions provided by your average driver's education course. With a fair amount of open road to cover between North Carolina and their home in Spring, Texas (a suburb of Houston), Jack and Linn began to think long and hard about applying the lessons he had learned as an autocross driver and instructor to creating a serious one-day program to help teenagers drive safely within their natural limits, as well as limits imposed by road conditions, the quality of their automobile, and the skills of the other drivers on the road.

When Linn and he began talking about driver safety and how it related to teens, Jack said, he began pondering the sobering reality that 47 percent of accidents involving teenagers are single vehicle accidents, in which the driver loses control of the car and hits an immovable object—a parked car, a tree, a telephone pole. The crash rate per mile for teen drivers is about *four times* higher than that for adults. "I began to think about creating a program that would be post driver's ed, a course that would teach teens to control their cars by bringing them into these real-life situation, like skids or an opposing vehicle, in a safe, controlled environment." By the time he and Linn had driven into their driveway in Spring, Jack—encouraged and supported in this endeavor by his wife, who did not dismiss it as off-the-wall, unrealizable, or a pipe dream—had dug the foundation, built half the wall, and hoisted the ramparts of his castle into the sky.

"The idea came to me clear as a bell," Jack told me proudly on the phone later that week, which was paying himself a real compliment because Jack is one of those highly competent, well-applied people who values clarity above just about everything else. "The idea was this: a Teen Car Control School." Without spending a lot of time trying to think up some fancy name for the program, before the week was out, he had registered the domain name, TeenCarControlSchool.com, and was off and running—

not to the races, but to the parking lots, horse racetracks, abandoned airfields, sports stadiums, flea markets, and other places not typically open every day of the week. For his locations, he could use almost any large paved area lacking obvious obstructions such as light, utility, or telephone poles.

Jack's Teen Car Control castle spoke directly to me because it connected to my own hopes as well as deepest fears. In our society, our notions of risk are often seriously skewed by emotion, as well as by the media. We fear pesticide residues on apples that carry an infinitesimally small cancer risk, but we let our kids hit the streets, highways, and byways by the thousands with virtually no preparation for what they might find when they get there late at night, in bad weather, with drunken and unsafe and reckless drivers out on the roads. Jack's car control school embodied the same notion that his daughter and I had been discussing before—the value of taking calculated risks and accumulating the skills so that you can learn to live life with a smile.

Egged on by my strong conviction that as *urgent* as his job search was, pursuing this idea was vitally *important*, Jack became more seriously involved in the succeeding weeks in translating his vision into reality. Through my connection, Jack called up Skip Barber and discovered that, to his dismay, he had recently sold both his racing and driving schools and was no longer formally involved with the program. But they did discuss a number of the steps Skip had taken to get his school off the ground. Immediately, Jack began to think about the differences between Skip Barber's school and his own program, which he had begun actively refining and developing with a partner, Randy Everson, a longtime teacher at car control schools in the Chicago area, who had developed some unique materials and techniques for teaching safe driving in a controlled environment.

Skip Barber's driving schools are relatively expensive and time-consuming undertakings, so Jack began to think creatively about cutting down costs and time. He became convinced that it was important to have the students drive their own cars as opposed to a fleet of specially prepared cars, equipped with costly additional controls and brakes—not just to save money but "because learning on one car and driving another in real life can be quite a switch."

Jack's next concrete step was to set up a meeting with the Topeka-based Sports Car Clubs of America (SCCA), a non-profit organization. While they were none too sure about endorsing or partnering with a for-profit organization, they were sufficiently impressed with Jack's presentation that when *another* writer for the *Wall Street Journal* called the SCCA looking for information about teen safety and driver's education, Jonathan Welsh, the head of the organization told him without hesitation, "You've got to talk to Jack Smyth—he's the leading teen car control guy in the country. He's got that corner covered."

"That was certainly an impetus to get my Web site up and running," Jack later told me, laughing. Jack's idea suddenly began to gain momentum rapidly. When it seemed to be miraculously circulating in the ether around us, I told him the wonderful story of the One Hundred Monkeys. It is a story about tipping points and about how ideas become infectious, like viruses.

In 1952, on the island of Koshima in Japan, scientists began feeding a strain of indigenous monkey, known by its Latin name *Macaca fuscata*, raw sweet potatoes dropped in the sand. The monkeys found that they liked the taste of raw sweet potatoes, but they also found that the dirt covering them was none too pleasing to their palettes. One day, an eighteen-month-old female named Imo found that she could solve this problem by washing her potatoes in a nearby stream. She taught this trick to her mother, as well as her playmates, who taught their mothers too.

Between 1952 and 1958, the astonished scientists who had been observing the behavior of these monkeys in the wild on Koshima for many years were witness to a virtual epidemic of potato washing. Curiously, only the adults who imitated their children—who had learned from Imo—picked up on this new simian fashion, while the other adults kept eating the dirty sweet potatoes. By the autumn of 1958, a comparatively high percentage of the monkeys on Koshima had learned to wash their sweet potatoes. But then an even stranger phenomenon occurred. The acquired habit of washing food before eating mysteriously leapt over the sea to infect colonies of monkeys on neighboring islands. Scientists could only conclude that when a certain critical number of monkeys learned that washing sweet potatoes was a good idea, this tipping point may somehow be communicated by, as it were, osmosis.

While Jack waited for the proverbial hundredth monkey to start washing her sweet potatoes—for his Teen Car Control School idea to take off like a rocket and soar—he became acutely aware that his severance package provided him with compensation and outplacement services for only six months. After that, he was on his own. Early on in a search process that was taking far longer than he had initially anticipated, his natural optimism and confidence still sustained him. I rarely, if ever, detected resignation in his voice. But as the months wore on, and on, and more and more leads and prospects failed to pan out, the harsh reality of his situation began to dawn on him.

The more he thought about what he had really enjoyed in the past, the more he began to recall with wistful nostalgia the rough sensibility and feeling of surprise and engagement that infused a number of the brash young startups he had nourished as a young man in the early days of Silicon Valley. One of which—the Learning Company—would later be sold for a couple of billion bucks to Mattel, which, in a debacle that cost Mattel CEO Jill Barad her job, was later sold for a song after suffering a long string of losses. He decided to focus, to the degree it was practicable, on interviewing with young, small startups that would ideally be infused with the freshness and sense of discovery and possibility that had gotten lost while he faithfully and devotedly worked his way up the corporate ladder at a succession of larger companies.

He was willing to take a 50 percent cut in compensation—including pay and other bonuses and incentives—for what he considered the "right" job, which he defined as one with long-term growth potential. His number one priority was finding a job that he would enjoy more than his work in a big corporation. He was eager, even hungry, to return to his entrepreneurial roots, but the great stumbling block in that quest turned out to be the challenge of persuading prospective employers that he was essentially entrepreneurial in spirit. His entrepreneurial activities were, by computer industry standards, ancient history—seventeen years in the past. He found that he had difficulty "casting himself against type."

As his severance clock began to run out, Jack and I put more time into developing a technique for dealing with the inevitable rejections of the job seeker: not taking things personally. When last month's hot prospects had called back and said, apologetically, "Sorry, Jack, but I think we're looking to take the company in a different direction," he had to force himself to realize that *it was not about him, it was about them.*

Jack learned this lesson the hard way when he flew himself all the way to Philadelphia to interview with a company that had posted a job for a regional sales manager in the Texas/Southwest region. He had undergone three excellent interviews on the phone with, among other senior staffers, the vice president of sales, who, after murmuring a number of encouraging words, informed Jack that he'd like to set up just one more major phone interview—a conference call with a top management group—before reaching a final decision.

This felt like a defining moment for Jack. This was the point at which, on the spur of the moment, he decided to take a stand. "No, I don't want to do things that way," he said, in a way that made it clear that he wasn't going to take no for an answer. "I'd much rather come out there and speak to you in person. My brother lives just outside of Philadelphia, so it's no big problem for me to pay my own way to come present myself to you face-to-face." To take a stand at that point meant that even if he didn't land the position, he would be able to say to himself that he hadn't left any stone unturned on the way. Jack understood that there remained some hesitancy on their part about filling the position at all, because the firm did not do much business in the Texas/Southwest region. They were skeptical that there was a major market there for their products and services.

Anticipating precisely this problem, Jack sat down and very carefully put together a list of prospective accounts and contacts in his area, and a fully fleshed-out game plan of how he intended to sell the company's products and services to them. But he knew he had a problem when he turned up in their reception area only to be apologetically informed by the VP of sales that the founder of the company and CEO couldn't make it in that day because she was home sick. He thought to himself immediately, "Is she really home sick? Or does she just not want to meet me?" During his visit to the company, he got the distinct impression that the VP of sales was locked in a power struggle with the founder and head of the company and that while he wanted to take the risk and hire Jack, she wasn't buying it. His sole consolation, after having put himself through this intensely frustrating experience, was that the obstructions being placed in his path were so obviously *all about them, not about him*. Shortly after his return to Texas, he got the phone call he had been expecting from the VP of sales, telling him the by-now-familiar refrain: they had decided to take the company in a different direction and wouldn't be requiring the services of a regional sales manager in his area.

The fact that this assertive—as opposed to aggressive—strategy didn't happen to work in that particular situation does not mean that he shouldn't have given it a shot. His approach turned out to be irrelevant to the outcome. But it did make a difference in his sense of himself and his own situation. Rather than waiting for them to take action or give him direction, he acted as a leader, and he acted the hard-driving salesman that he is. In the end, transcending the victim role mattered more to him than the position itself.

Several weeks later, he was actively pursuing a position with a major software company. He had once again gone through the seemingly requisite three interviews, when on his final interview he spoke out quite frankly about what a major undertaking it would be to have whoever ended up filling this newly created post deliver on its potential. The real issue, he insisted, in filling this position was whether the company could support that person to a degree that would permit him or her to succeed.

Even when faced with the probability that he was talking himself out of a job, Jack would have preferred to remain unemployed than put himself into any situation where he might end up—through no fault of his own—falling flat on his face. At one point, he took a consulting job that required him to evaluate the potential for a hardware company to set up a dealer network. The job was offered to him with the distinct understanding that if the answer to all of management's questions were yes, he would be offered the position of vice president of dealer sales, in charge of creating and managing a national network of independent hardware resellers. But after studying the company carefully and the competitive space it was attempting to move into, he regretfully concluded—much as it pained him to say so—that the company had not yet reached that stage in its own evolution to support such a national network. You might call it cutting off your nose to spite your face. But the way he saw it, this was maturity, this was taking a stand, this was saying that no matter how firmly his back was up against a wall, there were some things he just wouldn't do, some places he just wouldn't go. His defining moment had arrived.

Some nights when he couldn't sleep, he started mulling over the statistics. You know the ones I mean. The ones they print in all the magazines during a slow news cycle, when they announce with the ring of truth that "one in five people over thirty-five who aren't married will never get married and have kids." Or "one in three people fired over fifty will never get a job, so they should hang it up right now." I am, by the way, making these numbers up to illustrate a point, which is that the *statistics don't matter*. If you believe the statistics and accept them as "facts," they become self-fulfilling prophecies. As I told Senator Bob Graham when that silly young man showed him the negative article on his laptop computer before the debate, "There are some things that just need to get edited out." With Jack, I said, "These statistics are all about the past, not the future." Jack Smyth became rather skilled at editing out those voices of doom and gloom, although at times—often past three A.M.—it took some real mental discipline.

Then one day out of the blue, just as Jack was beginning to really wonder when it would all end, an old friend from Compaq named Bob Jackson called and told him that he had a new company called Spring Medical System, which was headquartered, miraculously enough, in Jack's own home town of Spring, Texas. Even more miraculously, it was located in his subdivision. Spring Medical had everything that he had been seeking from his first day off the job. It was young, it was brash, and it was small. If Bob hired Jack, he would be its sixth employee. Bob told Jack that when he had called a few people in the industry to describe the job—which involved helping to set up a national dealer network to sell software packages and services to medical offices—

just about every person Bob consulted had said, "The person you need is Jack Smyth." It wasn't that there were two or three people on their list. There was one.

Jack and Bob entered into negotiations during that conversation and very quickly came to an agreement that both could live with. At ten minutes to one on December 2, 2003, Jack and Bob had a deal. By one, ten minutes later, Jack was on his first conference call in his new position. He made his first presentation to several hundred dealers in Phoenix on January 19, and it was a smashing success. Dealers were crawling all over themselves to sign up with Spring Medical.

Looking back Jack says that he believes that the key lesson he learned from his nearly year and a half out in the cold was "the importance of having a sustaining vision to get you through the dark valleys. The importance of building that castle. A key part of the castle construction process is translating that vision into reality. Sometimes it's important to keep your eyes focused on that more distant horizon, while pursuing the less thrilling but no less important goal of finding a job."

With the urgent need of steady employment at last taken care of, Jack discovered that, to his delight, his job had been fueling—as opposed to obscuring—his dream. Having finally found a job that he enjoys enormously and that partially fulfills his entrepreneurial desires, he is no less devoted to getting his dream castle off the ground. You might be wondering what happened to the Teen Car Control School. Jack found that the liability insurance required to operate the school was prohibitively expensive, so he has changed the focus to working with car clubs associated with major manufacturers—BMW, Porsche, Audi—to have his organization run teen car control schools under their auspices, for the benefit of their members. That way, he can piggyback on their existing insurance policies and get his school up and running.

Jack's often harrowing experience attempting to build two castles simultaneously is the embodiment of a passage I truly treasure, describing the inestimable power of commitment and conviction:

> There is one elementary truth, the ignorance of which kills countless ideas and splendid plans. *The moment one definitely commits oneself, then Providence moves too.* All sorts of things occur to help one that would never otherwise have occurred . . . Whatever you can do or dream you can, *begin it.* Boldness has genius, power and magic to it. *Begin it now.*
>
> —Johann Wolfgang von Goethe

Exercise One: Embrace Flexibility

Imagine yourself as nimble, dancing, at one with the flux. There are very few sports in which it doesn't benefit you to stay light on your feet. Let's say you ski, cycle, surf, play tennis, or play the guitar—all of these pursuits provide a practice arena for letting your body do what it already knows how to do, without permitting your mind to get in the way. Scott Hamilton summed it up very well when Jim McKay interviewed him during the 2002 Winter Olympics. McKay asked the veteran figure skater what he's thinking about when he does a triple axel. "Think? You don't think about anything. You do it. If you start thinking you'll get in the way of your body knowing. It's the training and the practice and the doing it over and over and over. And your faith and confidence in the instincts of your body." Later he said, "I tell myself, you have to skate stupid."

Exercise Two: Consider the Rightness of Being Blown off the Old Trapeze

These challenging moments often appear in our lives at precisely the right moment we are ready for them. Despite his secure position, Jack Smyth was ready to become an entrepreneur. In fact, he got two entrepreneurial opportunities for the price of one. When faced with what may seem at first sight like an unwelcome change, make a list of all the possible positive things that could come from it. And move forward with grace and ease.

Exercise Three: Ban Statistics

Make a list of all the statistics you've bought into over the years. Throw it out.

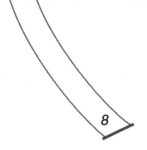

TWO LAWYERS FROM MANHATTAN

PART I: THE CASE OF THE DISAPPEARING ATTORNEY

ONE DAY IN THE FALL OF 2002, I received a call from a human resources executive at a large New York–based telecommunications company, who told me that one of their senior corporate counsels would be interviewing a handful of executive coaches over the next couple of weeks and was hoping to meet with me when it was convenient. Maggie Alexander's problem, as he explained it to me, was not that she wasn't smart. She was off-the-charts smart. It was not that she wasn't competent, because she was incredibly competent. In fact, it was precisely because the company thought so highly of her that they had determined that she would benefit enormously from a course of executive coaching.

A few of the issues that Maggie Alexander was struggling with had roots more in her physicality and her psychology. She stood five foot two inches in her stocking feet, looked to be about twenty-six years old, and tended to speak, particularly on the not infrequent occasions when she was nervous, in a high-pitched scratchy voice. Rather than develop a forceful, magnetic personality that might have overcome some of these natural imperfections, she had developed a self-effacing style that, if anything, only seemed to exacerbate them. I immediately conjured up an image of the classic "shy type," whose tendency to hide beneath a bushel basket might cause people to dismiss, overlook, or ignore her. Metaphorically at least, I thought of Maggie's dilemma as the Case of the Disappearing Attorney.

When we met at her Manhattan office, she had one of her three children with her, a cute little girl and a real little pistol who was having a ball playing at being a legal executive like her mom. It was immediately apparent that Maggie had no shortage of natural advantages. She is a natural beauty, with clear gray eyes, fine skin, and a pretty face. Yet at the same time she was— I think she'd admit it freely today—not doing all that much to accentuate the positive; if anything, her nondescript baggy suits, combined with her slouchy posture, tended to make her blend into the woodwork. Camouflage may be a fine defensive maneuver for animals and soldiers, but for lawyers, executives, and other civilians, it's usually better to stand out.

It's always interesting to pick a point of access into a new client's core issues. With Maggie, my access point was her posture. With a self-deprecating wince and a wave—indicating with her body language that she knew that she was truly undeserving—she laughingly said that of course she should stand up straighter and taller, but it was so hard to remember. When she forgot, she slouched.

"What sort of posture," I asked, "do you want your little girl to have when she grows up?"

"I want her to stand up straight and tall," she replied without thinking about it.

"The next time you catch yourself slouching," I suggested, "stand up for her."

That got her standing up straight as a telephone pole, in a hurry.

Another of the ways that Maggie's low self-esteem manifested itself was in her tendency to speak a little too quickly, rushing through her sentences so that a listener received the distinct impression that she didn't consider anything she was saying particularly worthwhile. "I know I'm a small person," she said, apologetically, "and that I look young," in a soft voice that simply confirmed what she was saying. "I know that the way I present myself hinders my growth, my moving up, but I'm just not sure what I can do about that."

She told me that on a recent trip to her husband's family home in Michigan, she had been asked to run out and pick up a six-pack of beer. Even with one of her three daughters in tow, she got carded. Not many thirty-six-year-old women would have been unhappy to have been carded by some kid at least ten years younger than she was, but Maggie was mortified. "I was standing there with my daughter saying 'Honestly sir, I *am* 21.'" He had to call the manager to confirm that her driver's license was not just a good fake.

From our introductory meeting I knew that what we had on our hands was what I like to call an Inside-Outside Makeover. The posture, the voice, the hair, the make-up, the clothes, the attitude, the self-concept, the works. I can't tell you how much I was looking forward to it. I love the whole idea of Inside-Outside Makeovers, particularly when I see the light in the newly-made-over person's eyes when she looks into a mirror and sees for the first time not only what she has become, but what she could be.

What made the prospect even more enticing in Maggie's case was that she was so obviously open to these new possibilities. Judging by her indifference to fashion, she might well have regarded the idea of getting a total Inside-Outside Makeover as the equivalent of a root canal. But I could tell from the first moment

I mentioned the possibility that she was utterly into it. Before we went from outer appearances to more interior changes, we would need to start carving the new her—Michelangelo-style—from the core. Surprisingly enough, she wasn't in the least bit intimidated by her peers. Only when interacting with her seniors, her superiors, and anyone she perceived as authority figures did she became tongue-tied and inarticulate, self-conscious, and committed to hiding herself, if possible, behind the nearest potted plant.

During our first working session, we took a few practical steps toward working on one aspect of that problem. We started working on her voice. I asked her to record and rerecord her answering machine message until the voice on the tape seemed deeper, stronger, surer, and warmer. I was intent on creating an answering machine "persona" that made anyone who dialed her number feel as though they had come to "the right place." Our goal was to induce in anyone, even a cold caller, the unassailable feeling that Maggie knew what she was talking about, that she cared about you, that she was going to take care of you, and most importantly, that she was going to *get the job done*. After I left, Maggie wrote a memo to her bosses.

I met with Gail today and we agreed upon the following objectives, which I will pursue in our upcoming meetings.

Improve my presentation/communications skills so that I:

• Have more effective content in my presentations.

• Consistently deliver informative, interesting, and motivating programs.

• Feel comfortable speaking in all group settings and with my communications skills in general.

You will soon see that we attained these objectives not by focusing so much on polishing or honing "communications skills" directly, but by concentrating on developing and evolving an entirely new Maggie from the elements of the old that she wanted to keep. This new Maggie would know how to communicate in ways that were naturally more effective and persuasive.

In our next session, we worked on one of her "From/To" lists.

1. From *I've got to show everyone that I know my stuff* to *I am an open, expansive person whom you can trust.*

2. From *Doing the homework (and showing you've done the homework)* to *Trusting myself and my natural skills so much that I can listen and respond to your needs.*

It didn't take long before we got close to the root of why she had become the "shy type."

"I was always such a big mouth at home," Maggie recalled, "and my parents used to say that around the house, they could never get me to shut up." But whenever she found herself in a new situation, a new camp, a new class, a new school, she became distinctly uncomfortable. She traced a great deal of her insecurity to the fact that when her mother said anything at all about her, it was always a variation on the theme, "You're worthless."

Maggie's mother came from a strict German family, where the parental disciplinary style was reflected in her father's reliance on a thick leather razor strop to keep his children in line. Although Maggie's mother had improved on her own parents' severe child-rearing methods, her unsupportive approach had left some pretty deep marks on her daughter's fragile self-esteem.

"Do you think your mother told you that to make you feel bad?" I asked her. Honestly, I didn't know the answer. I was simply searching for alternative interpretations to the most obvious one. At first, she didn't answer, so I tried again. "Do you think it's at all possible that your mother said that to motivate you, as opposed to demolish you?"

Maggie thought long and hard about that one before finally responding, as if trying the notion on for size. "Well, I suppose," she said with great hesitation, "it's possible that she said that to make me try harder."

From my point of view, the truth of the matter really didn't matter. The whole point of this exercise was to show her that it was *possible* that she could decide which way was up and which way was down in her life. I wanted her to try to open her mind to the possibility that her mother had told her she was worthless in a loving way, strange as that may sound. "If you're going to stay who you are, then there is every reason to believe in this truth, that your mother's disdain for you lies at the root of all of your problems. But let's consider the possibility, for the sake of argument, that your mother didn't really mean to diminish you, but to motivate you. Let's run with that, and see where it gets us."

In support of my position, I cited the examples of the often highly effective motivational philosophy espoused by the Marine Corps, army boot camps, and a good many collegiate and professional football teams, as well as (in my day at least) the prestigious Yale Drama School. I mentioned the basketball coach Bobby Knight, renowned for his loutish and brutish treatment of his players, which included hurling chairs at them on the court. The implicit message of the boot-camp school of coaching is that life is something at which you have to work hard. Coaches who adhere to this philosophy often tell players that they're worthless. "You're not worth my time," they like to say. "I'm ashamed to have you be a part of my team."

Needless to say, whenever I get the chance, I like to point out that this approach is often not very effective with teams, children, companies, or animals. I told Maggie the story of the senior executive at Avon who took pride in motivating the district managers, the true core of the company, by repeatedly telling them that they were not good enough, that they had fallen short, that their productivity left much to be desired, and that they had would just have to do better next time—or else. "I'm disap-

pointed in your performance," this executive would say in audio tapes he distributed to the entire group, who were aghast at how he abused them, mistreated them, and worst of all, misunderstood them. "I don't think you will get the results you are looking for using that approach," I would say, but he was insistent that it was effective. But what actually happened was that the district managers, the good ones, felt belittled and unappreciated, and their productivity went down, not up. Their attitude was, "How dare you? You don't even know how hard I work! Who do you think you are?" The executive never used that technique again.

Fortunately for Maggie, her company took a more supportive approach to executive training and development, more in the style of the beloved Phil Jackson of the Los Angeles Lakers, who asks his players for the moon but supports them every step of the way. Shortly after we began working together, Maggie had a meeting scheduled with all the senior executives in her business unit, to discuss the possible acquisition of another company. The meeting started out with all the participants introducing themselves to the group, and Maggie immediately began to worry, *Why would they possibly care who I am?* But then she focused on a particular item from her "From/To" list—From *I've got to show everyone that I know my stuff* to *I am an open, expansive person whom you can trust*—and introduced herself to the room without further incident.

It couldn't have been more than a couple of days later that she

found herself walking down a corridor in her office building, on her way to yet another meeting to discuss this potential acquisition, when she ran into her boss's boss, the general counsel, a very senior woman whom she highly respected yet was somewhat intimidated by. Rather than just casually asking her how the project they were working on was going, Maggie became very self-conscious and ended up saying nothing at all. "I thought I was prying into something that was none of my business and that she would have resented the intrusion," she later told me, explaining her paralysis. "You know, 'Who *is* this person?'"

As a way of stilling these negative voices in her head, I suggested that she seek confirmation of the positive voices all around her from people who loved her. I asked her to ask her husband, Roger, to make a list of all the qualities that he most valued, admired, and respected about her. He made a wonderful long list, but the item that most deeply touched Maggie's heart was when he wrote, at the end, "You are my soul-mate." She later realized that if she had never asked him to write down his feelings that way, he would never have expressed himself so poetically.

Maggie's sister, for her part, praised her for being such a "wonderful mother," who always displayed a great deal of patience with her children. "I would have thought," Maggie said later, "that since she'd heard me yell at my kids from time to time, and she knew that I worked hard at the office and wasn't at home as much as I would have liked to be, that she would never have said

that." Her sister added, for good measure, that she was grateful that Maggie was always there for her when she needed her.

I then asked her to think about people she admired. Without missing a beat, she named her boss, Linda, the associate general counsel, as the person she would most like to emulate. Linda was the sort of woman who could walk into a room and within a nanosecond, have everyone looking up to her and turning to her for advice. She had a quietly commanding presence and was one of those women who seem instinctively to know what to say at the right time, to be able to do what needed to get done without a lot of fuss and bother. "She's someone who can just get other people pumped up, in a good way," Maggie said.

She also spoke with genuine admiration of her mother-in-law, who, while not the professional type, was "a really smart woman who cares deeply about other people and is just genuinely nice and warm and supportive, yet at the same time, powerful. She has a way of making everybody else around her feel better about themselves." She was, in other words, in just about every way the polar opposite of Maggie's mother.

I urged her to take the lessons she had learned from interacting with her husband's family not only to recreate a similar atmosphere at home, but also at her office. One of the first tests of this new approach emerged when Maggie was asked to work on an acquisition. The team working on the deal was headed up by the chief of her company's corporate development, whom Maggie described as "one of those people I knew I was going to have to prove myself to." He was a naturally forceful person, who, if he were going to value her contribution to his team, would need to be persuaded that she had something of value to contribute. She decided, at my urging, to win him over. This wasn't about being manipulative or phony or "pulling the wool over someone's eyes," but simply speaking directly to him as one professional to another. She knew, in other words, that it was simply a case of letting the real Maggie sit up and shine.

In her earlier, less forceful incarnation, she would have perceived his cool professionalism as nothing but being given the cold shoulder. But rather than focus on how others were perceiving her—"Do they like me? Do they think I'm too young to handle this?"—she transferred her attention to her solemn commitment to serving the interests of her client, the company. What got her over this seemingly major hurdle was repeating the powerful Dorothy Sarnoff mantra, which I had asked her to memorize as homework following our first session: "I'm glad I'm here. I'm glad you're here. I care about you. I'm in control." That mantra helped to solidify her primary goal, which was to shift the attention away from herself to the commitment she had made to the company. What was most gratifying for Maggie was that after their return to headquarters, the chief of corporate development had made a point of telling her boss how glad he was that Maggie was on his team.

Not long thereafter, she found the perfect opportunity to use some of these same techniques in a different environment. Her town's PTA meeting. Being "the shy type," she was accustomed to sitting way in the back and saying nothing at these gatherings. After all, what could she possibly have to say that would make any difference? But at this next meeting, she had decided that she wanted to make a difference. I strongly suggested that rather than just throwing on a faded pair of jeans and an old sweater, that she put on some lipstick and a sharp pair of slacks and a nice sweater. On her way to the meeting, she ran into a drug store and stood for a few minutes before a rack of lipsticks, baffled by the multiplicity of choice on the shelves. She studied the different colors very intently, inevitably worried that she would make the wrong choice. Then, she started laughing at the absurdity of it all. Now, it was a woman in the same aisle's turn to be baffled.

"What's so funny?" the woman asked, smiling.

"I'm thirty-six years old," Maggie answered, barely able to contain herself, "and this is the first tube of lipstick I've ever bought in my life!"

Maybe it was the lipstick, maybe it was the slacks, maybe it was the light dusting of face powder, or the shoes, but by the time she stepped into that PTA meeting, it was the new Maggie standing there, ready to roll. The little group that ran the PTA was, like all such groups, determined not to brook any interference from outsiders. They were running the meeting with their typical heavy hand when out of the blue, Maggie realized that they were in the midst of voting down the annual end-of-school picnic for the kids.

The new Maggie wouldn't have it. "Excuse me," Maggie raised her hand, finally finding a voice that was warm, sure, and strong. "I'm sorry, maybe I missed something from a prior meeting, but are you really planning to eliminate the end-of-school picnic?"

They all looked terribly pained, and explained to her—as if to a child—that that was precisely what they were doing. Maggie, who had never before opened her mouth in their presence, ended up making a cogent legal argument in defense of the end-of-year picnic. It turned out, once somebody said something, that she had stirred up a palace revolt. Quite a few of the other parents at the meeting believed much the way as she did but felt too intimidated to speak out. Maggie had decided going into that meeting that not only would she assert her point of view, but she would be a unifying force as opposed to a divisive one. As a result of her calm, sure voice, the PTA board and the parents worked out a reasonable compromise, as opposed to a brawl. The funds were cut, but the picnic was saved. The following morning, one of the mothers who had attended the meeting but not spoken up called Maggie to thank her for what she had done. Maggie Alexander was, in her own mind at least, a little bit of a hero.

Not long after she bought her first tube of lipstick, we went for the full makeover. We started out at the John Barrett Salon, where she had her hair cut by David Evangelista, a famous fashion stylist who now performs makeover miracles on his own TV show. Before she went in, she was a bit afraid to getting made up. Not only had she never had makeup done professionally, she'd hardly ever worn any makeup at all. She was not the "made up" type. I told her that this was about bringing out a you that was always there, under the surface—not a fake you, a real you. One of many potential real yous. She had her makeup done by a wonderful makeup artist, Rachel, also at the John Barrett Salon, who not only made her up and shaped her eyebrows, but taught her how to do it all for herself at home and what products to buy. When we were done, David and Rachel pronounced her "Good to go," which was precisely how she felt: *good to go*, if not—with apologies to best-selling author Jim Collins—*From Good To Great*.

To help her shed her old slouchy suits, I made an appointment for her with Elaine Mack, one of the top personal shoppers at Bergdorf Goodman. Maggie arrived a little early for her appointment with Elaine, who said, "Why don't you go down to the Donna Karan show and check out her new fall line?"

Maggie wasn't so sure what she meant by "show," but she said okay, thinking that Elaine must be referring to the area in the store where the Donna Karan clothes were kept on display. "My assistant is down there," Elaine said. "You can't miss her: she's tall and very beautiful." So Maggie found her way down to the Donna Karan section, only to realize that there was a fashion event in progress. Loud music was playing and waiters in short white coats carried trays with finger foods and drinks. Maggie was utterly confused by all these people milling around. Maggie began looking at all the clothes on the racks—without price tags, which seemed strange. Suddenly she heard a fashionably dressed woman say to another customer standing nearby: "Oh, let me introduce you to Donna Karan."

"Good God," Maggie thought. "What am I doing here?" But then she thought to herself, "Why *shouldn't* I be here?" As the fashion show wound down, Elaine appeared and took her under her wing. Elaine Mack has a great eye, and she presented Maggie with several simple, elegant, and beautifully cut suits for her to choose from. Maggie selected a smashing black one that not only fit her beautifully on the outside, but befitted her new interior self as well.

When she went back to work, she wore her new Donna Karan suit, her new makeup, her new haircut, and her new shoes. Needless to say, she felt a little bit anxious and self-conscious about how all this newness was going to play at the office, although she had been somewhat reassured by the enthusiastic reaction of her husband, who had gotten an enormous kick out of the whole thing. After taking one look at her, he had only one question: "Wow! What's next?"

Still, Maggie had every reason to worry that some people might think she'd gotten a little bit full of herself, or was just putting on some sort of false front. Instead, the reaction from her colleagues was overwhelmingly positive. People all over her office were absolutely delighted and amazed. During a meeting, one of her colleagues sincerely apologized for not wearing his suit jacket, because she made him feel a little slouchy. That really cracked her up.

Her big turning point came several weeks later with a major meeting in Chicago to discuss the details of a new strategic alliance. Her boss had made a point of sending her out to this meeting because she had been most directly involved in working out the details of the deal. But the other company had brought their general counsel with them, and at one point the head of the team for the opposing party had said challengingly to the head of Maggie's team, "We've brought our general counsel. Could you tell us who will be in charge of the legal aspects from your side?"

The old Maggie would have slumped down in her chair, felt small, and remembered that she was nothing but a "lowly lawyer." But the new Maggie spoke up at once, in the same clear, calm voice that she now owned as surely as her new power suit. She didn't even wait for the team head on her side to answer the question.

"I will be heading up the legal team for Grandstar Communications," she said firmly. And that was that.

PART II: THE CASE OF THE WRONGED ATTORNEY FOR WHOM TWO WRONGS DID MAKE A RIGHT

Roberta King's first job, right out of law school, was with the New York office of a major firm headquartered in Los Angeles. Roberta was a bit older than the typical first-year associate because she had worked for a few years between graduating from college and attending law school in California. She had been so excited about landing her first big-time job in the big city, that she plunged into her work, while also doing a bit of volunteering in her field, agreeing to serve as general counsel to a leading group of women in finance, as well as speaking to a number of professional groups that sought her expertise as an attorney specializing in certain arcane areas of banking and financial law.

But it became clear within her first few weeks on the job that things weren't working out with her boss, Polly, the manager of the banking and finance practice group of the firm's New York office. Their first encounters had been encouraging. Polly had the capacity to be extremely charming and engaging, when it suited her to be so. But other days, quite unpredictably, she would fly off the handle, throw temper tantrums, and denounce Roberta mercilessly, in the bluntest and harshest terms.

"You're not growing properly here," she might say, or—

apropos of nothing—"I'm not sure that you really fit in." Some days, the problem was that Roberta was "behind the eight ball." On other days, her fault seemed to be that she was "lacking in leadership qualities." On still other days, she just didn't seem to be acquiring the "skill set" that she needed to truly flourish at the firm. Whatever it was, Roberta wasn't—in her view—measuring up, and as Roberta later expressed it to me, "In New York City, when you're working all the time, there seems to be no refuge from work, where you can regain some perspective on what's going on in your office."

Roberta felt miserable most of the time, and she felt that she owed her acute distress to her abysmal relationship with her boss. Of the many things that terrified Roberta, the most terrifying were Polly's frequent dark references to a performance review that was always said to be *in the offing*, but never in fact came to pass. All of her fellow junior associates got their reviews, but not Roberta, who received the distinct impression that her boss, for some mysterious reason, would prefer to hold her dreaded review over her head, rather than lose it as leverage.

As the months turned into years, Roberta became increasingly fixated on pleasing her boss, who simply refused to be pleased. What was even more confusing for Roberta was the fact that Polly was so utterly mercurial—sweet one day, ice cold the next, almost as if she were dealing with distinct personalities. Simply as a survival strategy, Roberta began seeking out more productive relationships with other senior attorneys in her office, a number of whom seemed to take a shine to her and find ways to give her assignments.

One of these extra-departmental connections led to her being assigned to work on a case for a major client, the majority of whose legal work was customarily handled out of the main Los Angeles office. Roberta immediately hit if off with the client's in-house counsel, who was in charge of distributing the client's case load. When a new piece of work came in from this particular client, the in-house counsel made a special point of asking for Roberta to be assigned to the case. When informed of this request, however, Roberta's boss simply replied that Roberta was far too busy on other things to take on this additional load. But the client, in this case, as clients can, simply overruled Roberta's boss and insisted that the assignment be given to Roberta.

"That one event, seemingly minor as it was, meant the world to me, because it confirmed that I was not entirely worthless," Roberta later told me. For obvious reasons, she was beginning to lose faith in herself. Roberta began throwing herself into this case, working on weekends and nights. She even canceled her vacation to get the work completed on schedule, by which time she had fallen seriously ill. Sick as she was, she hauled herself into the office once the case was officially completed to tie up a couple of loose ends. The minute she saw her, and as sick as she was, her boss marched her into her office as if she were a kid she'd caught playing hooky, and told her in the coldest voice imaginable that she "simply wasn't wired to do this sort of work."

At this low point in Roberta's work life, Polly fired her on the spot.

That was pretty much when I entered into the picture, after Roberta had been kicked after she was down. Her firm had in its generosity granted her six months to find a new job, during which she was permitted to keep her office and her secretary, while the fact that she had been dismissed was supposed to be kept a secret. How well kept a secret was anybody's best guess. The firm had fired her in an unusually tough job market, one of the hardest lawyers of her age had encountered in years. Where just a few years before, at the peak of the boom, firms had eagerly lured new recruits with fat bonuses and hefty salaries and bloated benefits packages, now they could afford to be choosy. The way that Roberta put it was that many of them were just window-shopping, in the sense that while they might post an opening on a Web site or in a professional journal, the reality was that they would only decide to fill that position if a candidate really blew them away.

Right off the bat, we concentrated on giving her a fresh start emotionally. "I had been told in the most blunt and unpleasant terms that I was lacking and that I was at fault," she stated frankly during one of our first sessions together. What we had to do now was laboriously reassemble a productive new self from the tattered remnants of the old. In terms of Taking the Ground

She'd Already Traveled, and in asking herself the question, "What does *great* look like?" I encouraged her to construct her dream life. I here provide a few tantalizing excerpts from her notes:

> I am fully in command of what I do. I understand the subject I am dealing with so well that I am truly an expert, and people (colleagues and clients) perceive my expertise. I feel confident in my ability to handle any problem or issue that may come up, regardless of whether it's something I've confronted before.
>
> I am not afraid of seeing things I've never seen before.
>
> My clients are loyal to me. Clients tell their friends about me and see me as the expert in my area. They invite me to join their team when they need my expertise.
>
> There is a market for what I know.
>
> I do not back down when challenged but continue to think clearly and articulate my own vision and thoughts.
>
> I am not afraid to have other people count on me.
>
> I can hold my own on the golf course.

I asked her to write down a few defining moments. Here is a severely abridged version of what she wrote:

> Childhood.
>
> Unpredictable, chaotic home life. I chose to be the peacemaker, caretaker for my sisters, placate my mother, tried to control the chaos.

Theme: take the path of least resistance, avoid trouble, control chaos, no home base or safe place.

Sound familiar? You know, what really interested me most about that last passage was that it gave us some solid ground from which to move forward. As I fully expected, when she spoke of how well she handled her clients, while inventorying her strengths, she mentioned that she always approached clients as if she were the quintessential Big Sister. By which she meant that in her clients' presence, she felt an overwhelming desire to take care of them, to control the chaos around them, to make them feel that she could create a safe place for them, and that she could make sure to keep danger and threatening forces at bay. I wrote a note to myself: *She has the capacity to make other people feel safe, warm, and welcome. What a uniquely fabulous trait for a lawyer!*

This was the safe Ground She'd Already Traveled. We were going to run well with that. We concentrated on preparing her for her job interviews, as this was clearly the most urgent task at hand. Given the terrible state of the job market, she was going to have to really ace those interviews if she was going to have even the slightest chance of landing a halfway decent job, let alone something terrific.

Roberta is a very attractive young woman, with a tendency to scowl between sentences. We worked hard on eliminating that scowl, which of course had been placed there for a good reason.

And we worked equally hard on persuading her to let go of the fact that yes, she had been right and they had been wrong. Really wrong. "Okay," I would say, "you're right. And that and a token will get you a ride on the subway."

Letting go of her need to be right about their being wrong was a difficult assignment for Roberta, given the vindictive behavior of her boss. One remark that continued to ring in Roberta's ears long after its deceptively disarming delivery was, "You know, Roberta, the fact that you are so awfully good with the clients is actually to your detriment, because it gives them the very false impression that you are far more capable than you actually are."

Polly was the Chris Evert of the backhanded compliment. She had succeeded in turning one of Roberta's greatest strengths—her engaging personality—into a perceived liability. But what Roberta immediately thought to herself—but didn't say—when she heard Polly's dagger-like comment was, "Now that's strange, because cozying up to the client and then letting them down is exactly what people here say about you!"

A psychologist would call it projection. I would call it cruel and unusual punishment. One of the first things that I ever said to Roberta was that sometimes we inadvertently step on other people's toes by encroaching upon their territory, and that seems to have been what had happened in this case. If this woman saw herself as a true client-pleaser, she may well have defensively re-acted to Roberta's client-pleasing skills by attempting to squelch them, or if she couldn't squelch them, by attempting to squelch her.

When we spoke about her childhood, Roberta told me with a certain degree of sad resignation in her voice that when she had told her parents she was planning to go to law school, their only response was, "Really? How are you planning to pay for it?"

"I hail from a family of underachievers," Roberta said with a rueful laugh. As a result of this difficult childhood, she had internalized an image of herself as fighting an uphill battle, every day, often in competition with people who had had it easy all of their lives and had no idea how much she had had to struggle to get to where she was today.

Deprived of any financial or emotional support from her parents—unless you count the chance remark that her mother once made when she caught her daughter studying hard for an exam, which was that there really wasn't any point to working hard because she could always get by on her looks—Roberta applied to law school three times before she was finally accepted. And the way that she got accepted was that after being waitlisted by the school she was hoping to attend in California, she drove out there without an appointment and demanded to meet with the admissions committee, which she simply informed that she was planning to attend—no ifs, ands, or buts about it.

She attended law school at night while working days to support herself. Despite the crippling hours, she graduated close to the top of her class, with honors. By the time she graduated, she had received two offers from major white-shoe law firms. But the one she had finally accepted had just about destroyed her fragile self-esteem.

As part of the process of Letting Go, she drew up a list of Throw Aways.

Number one was her "Polly Plant"—a plant given to her by her toxic boss. I suggested that she toss it into the trash using a thick pair of rubber gloves. Number two on her list was a litigation briefcase that had been given to her by a colleague and friend and loyal supporter who had been let go a few months before she was, in which she had dumped the records of a case she would rather forget—one that her boss had assigned to her without providing sufficient staff, which as a result had turned into a nightmare.

As it turned out, going out on that difficult job search at that difficult time was one of the most liberating things Roberta ever did in her life. It gave her the opportunity to free herself from the shackles of the past, and present a new bright face to the world. The best way to present her best self to the world was to think long and hard about the challenges she had already faced and overcome, so that she could more easily overcome similar challenges whenever they were placed in her path.

One of the first lawyers she interviewed with said, about halfway into their first meeting, "You must be *great* at getting new business."

To which she unhesitatingly replied, "You bet I am."

Roberta ended up receiving three wonderful job offers, in a market softer than Carvel ice cream. In all three cases, her prospective employers had said pretty much the same thing to her: "It isn't as if you've got the *exact* experience you need to do the job we want you to fill. But what we do know is that you've got the ability to gain that experience, and we're interested in supporting you while you do that."

Six weeks before the day this book went to press, Roberta moved to Chicago. She doesn't know a soul there and loves the idea of living in a new city where she can create a new self, and no one will be the wiser. From worthlessness to worthiness was her route. At her new job, her colleagues seem genuinely respectful and caring and concerned about her. More than once, and with apparent sincerity, people at her new firm have actually taken the trouble to pull her aside and tell her how happy they are to have her there and what a great job she's been doing.

"My entire interactions with people, on all sorts of levels," she reported to me recently with palpable pride, "seem to be predicated on radically different premises. Here, they seem to be genuinely interested in how I am doing and genuinely hoping for me to succeed."

One of her very first assignments was to review a complex agreement, the language of which was utterly unfamiliar to her. She had never seen an agreement quite like it, and partly because it was so novel, she took it back to her office and read it very closely, as if it were a novel, as opposed to a cut-and-dry legal boilerplate. She found that she had all sorts of problems with this agreement, including some of the basic assumptions on which the majority of its clauses seem to have been based. She marked up the whole document heavily and took it the next morning into her boss's office, who was somewhat taken aback at the density of her suggested revisions, particularly on a document she regarded as entirely routine. Leafing carefully through what Roberta had written, she minutely scrutinized every note in the margin, occasionally scribbling notes of her own on a legal pad, and nodding and chuckling as she went.

"Sometimes," she told Roberta when she was finished, "it really does pay to assign someone to a case who has no familiarity with the subject. Because you're dead right about the problems with this one, and quite frankly, if they'd given it to me, because I've seen a million like it, I'd have let most of this document slip by without thinking twice about it."

"Glad to be of help," the new Roberta said. That was all that she really needed to say. When I heard that story, I recalled the time that my father and I drove down for the first time to Sweetbriar College in Lynchburg, Virginia. I was more than a little nervous on the way down, and I kept asking my father to tell me all the best things he could think of about me. After he'd listed quite a few, I said, "Okay, can you tell me again?" He never once lost patience with me or told me to shut up, or even worse, to keep a stiff upper lip. Instead, he left me with two pieces of advice I'll never forget:

"Trust your instincts." And

"Nothing is irrevocable."

I told that story to Roberta King, who now knew far better than she had ever known to trust her instincts, because nothing is irrevocable. "I think," she told me recently, "that if I hadn't gone through that traumatic experience, I never would have learned to appreciate all of the really positive influences I have on other people. I would have taken them for granted, instead of valuing them for what they really are."

But what I treasured most from our experience together was when she said:

"Whenever I walk into a room and hold out my hand and say, confidently, 'Hello, I'm Roberta King,' that means something utterly different from what it meant before." Now, when she enters a room, there is no mistaking who she is. There's a whole new woman who goes by the name of Roberta King, for whom the question "How good can we make it?" can sincerely be answered, "As good as it gets."

For now.

Exercise: Finding Your Voice

Most people don't listen to themselves. In conversation, on tape, on TV, and on the rare occasions when they do, they tend to be shocked at what they hear. It sounds like someone else's voice. Which raises the question: What do you want people to hear when you speak? Your voice can define you more vividly than almost anything else about you. People whose looks don't stand out in a crowd can, if their voices are distinctive, come across as exceedingly compelling and even magnetic. Let your voice project the person you want to be.

One of the easiest ways to monitor your voice—and its effectiveness—is to listen closely to your answering machine or voice mail message. Is it inviting? Is it warm? Is it rich and resonant? Does it project the impression to callers that they are in good hands, that this is a person who cares? When they call you, whom have they called? You get to decide. Here's how: Listen closely, and critique yourself. Listen to your friends' messages. Rerecord your message several times, and then after a week, listen to it again—if possible, with new ears. When you watch TV or go to the movies, close your eyes for a moment and listen for the voices that you find really appealing. Imitate the sounds that you like. Once again, you get to decide what you sound like.

EPILOGUE

SO HERE WE ARE ONCE AGAIN, still under the big top, still in awe of those rare and wonderful trapeze artists who soar through the air with the greatest of ease, who, when they fall, bounce back so gracefully because they never let life's rough edges trim their sails—because they approach every new challenge with a sense of levity and an intuitive grasp that the human condition is, at best, a game.

Then there are the rest of us. There we sit beneath the big tent, gazing up in ardent and abject admiration at the sublime creatures who seem so effortlessly capable of letting go of their old trapezes and floating through the air into their next phase, without looking back with regret or remorse.

In the preceding pages, I introduced you to eight people—four men and four women—who are not aerialists but ordinary people caught for a variety of reasons between trapezes, who couldn't have come from a greater variety of backgrounds, life situations, or personal challenges. With their wildly disparate backgrounds and experiences, all of the heroes featured here share one common trait: Each one came to me fiercely committed to change. Not until actually writing this book did I truly appreciate the many striking, even uncanny, parallels between these separate lives. All of which provides confirmation that in so many ways, we are not alone. We are not isolated in our fears, our dreams, our passions, our convictions, our humor, our capacity to give, love, and grow.

We met Eileen Ast, who suffered the double blow of a husband's illness and the loss of a job, only to find her future through the art of self-reinvention in an ideal new professional position, combined with an enhanced family life. We encountered Senator Bob Graham, facing up to the daunting challenge of transforming himself from a senator into a president, discovering through the process of trapeze swinging an entirely new self within, as well as a new definition of leadership that made his devotion and commitment to his country more important than coming in first in the party horse race. We followed jazz guitarist Peter Mazza as he revised an overly narrow definition of what success looked like and realized that his true quest and calling lay not in chasing that big record deal but in discovering his own signature style, which would one day yield the deal he was looking for and create the fabulous future he knew he was destined to create.

For Andres Serrano, the philosopher in the enemy camp, the one searing lesson he was obliged to learn—even when it was painful—was that as a highly valued, if misunderstood, executive, it was incumbent upon him to discover the power within him to rise above an adverse situation, to take what had been objectively a pretty raw deal and find the diamond in the lump of coal. Anne Stanton's great challenge became to truly trust her instincts that she is in every conceivable way the absolutely right person in the right job at the right time. Jack Smyth lost his job, but gained a life. Even after finding a new job, Jack found that he had discovered something greater on the path to his next trapeze, a dream that taps into the talent that matters most deeply to him—his capacity and commitment to start something new in the world that will make a lasting difference in society and very likely will save countless young lives in the process. Maggie Alexander found her voice and, in the process, discovered an entirely new, far more confident, self-assured, and powerful self, one like the women she deeply admired. Like Eileen Ast and Jack Smyth, Roberta King lost a job and ironically, ended up gaining something far greater by enduring her short-term loss. Not only did she find a terrific new job in a terrific new city, but a terrific new life, which she can celebrate as a release from the abusive situation that forced her to confront her old self and create a new one—a self who would never stand for what she had been put through.

These eight people all learned to build their castles, to ask what great would look like, to wonder how good they could make it, and to let go of those things that caused them to perpetually pull back, as opposed to perpetually press forward. I came to deeply admire all of these people as we worked through their deepest, darkest, most difficult issues. Remarkably, all succeeded in their quests for self-realization. I do not pat myself on the back for their successes so much as feel awed by the intelligent, forceful, and imaginative ways that they took back their lives and took control of their destinies. They forged futures for themselves that enlarged, enhanced, broadened, and deepened their lives, as opposed to diminishing or lessening them.

It is no exaggeration to say that I feel truly blessed to have worked with these brave people, as well as the many others whose stories have yet to be committed to paper. In the first chapter, I talked about the importance of defining moments. One of the most critical insights we can have, a vital key to the process that unlocks those trapped souls within us and reveals our true selves to ourselves, is that it is we who have the capacity to decide who we are and what we are going to become, not anyone else. It is we who create our defining moments. It is we who truly define who we are as opposed to others' often narrower visions of our capabilities.

In every chapter, I have shown you people who are awfully smart, who possess expertise to spare, who know what they know but feel something lacking in how they present who they are to the world. But what started out, in many cases, as a problem of personal presentation became very quickly a matter of self-realization. It is not what we know that matters nearly so much as how deeply we care, and what we care about. That we all have castles to build is the ultimate point here. And if we don't build them, who will? Don't we owe it to ourselves to grasp the fullness and richness of our dreams, to not let the harshness, tenseness, and frequent unfairness we see all around us rudely rip our dreams and our hopes from our grasp? When faced with these arduous and daunting tasks, don't we all tend to shrink from the challenges that lie ahead and consider hiding or running or forgetting who we are and where we need to go? Of course we do, because we are only human.

In depicting real human beings in real life situations, undergoing often complex personal transformations and reinventions, I have had one goal in mind: to demonstrate with a level of proof rarely available to the scientist that yes, we can do it, that yes, we can all win. The knowledge that we do possess the tools to open the black boxes that constitute our remote and mysterious selves helps us to cope with our daily lives with levity, passion, courage, and dignity. It is this great knowledge that gives us confidence, that provides us with our voices, that compels us to step up to the plate, that permits us to walk into the arena, to seize the day, to force every moment to its pinnacle, to not just survive, but to prevail.

The true message here is not about merely living our lives, but about leaping through the present and soaring into an uncertain future with jaunty smiles on our faces. It's about discovering the fabulous feeling that every door lies open to us, that every window has been flung open to let in the sunshine from this wonderful world stretching before us into the distance, like some infinite landscape in a dream. Despite all the insecurity, pain, and baffling complexity that we face today, there has never been a better time to seize the moment, to realize that we *are* the right person, to perceive with new eyes that we are destined for greatness—as long as we are willing to let go of those familiar trapeze bars and swing into the next bright day that awaits us, soaring to meet our new selves in all their blazing glory.

So go ahead. Take that leap. You've got some flying to do.

There *is* no way it is.

There's only the way you say it *is*.

The Universe hasn't made up its mind about you.

It only knows what you show it today.

You are the Inventor.

Your life is the Invention.

You get to make it up.

So make it up good.

—Gail Blanke

Between Trapezes is only the beginning. We are actively encouraging all readers to join a growing community of "trapeze artists" who are longing to reinvent their work, their lives, and themselves. Every trapeze artist has a *catcher*, someone who reaches out and grasps his or her hands at precisely the right moment and lifts the artist onto the next trapeze. I invite you to log on to **www.betweentrapezes.com** and join our community of "flyers and catchers" who will help support your own particular journey "in between" with expertise and affection . . . and grasp *your* hands at exactly the right moment. You'll take courage from other people's stories, share your own, and receive ongoing coaching from me and my team of experts. Join us.

ABOUT THE AUTHOR

Gail Blanke has never met a person she couldn't motivate. In 1995, after helping to inspire Avon's million-person sales force to exceed expectations year after year and creating the Avon Breast Cancer Awareness Crusade, she created Lifedesigns as a division of Avon, specializing in empowerment workshops for working women. Two years later, she wrote the best-selling *In My Wildest Dreams: Living the Life You Long For* and became one of the most sought-after motivational speakers in the country. In addition to a solo appearance on *The Oprah Winfrey Show*, Gail has appeared on CNN, FNN, CNBC, and Fox TV and has been the subject of feature articles in *Newsweek, Business Week, Ladies' Home Journal*, the *Wall Street Journal, Redbook*, and *Self*.

Gail is a recipient of the Women Who Make a Difference Award, presented at the 1999 International Women's Forum Conference; the 1994 Matrix Award for Public Relations, presented by New York Women in Communications; and the 1994 Star Award, presented by the New York Women's Agenda. In 2003, she was named president of the New York Women in Communications Foundation, which provides college and graduate school scholarships for young women interested in careers in the communications industry. Gail lives in New York City with her husband, F. James Cusick, a writer, and their two daughters, Kate and Abigail.